A SHOT OF POISON

Christopher Long

All rights reserved under article two of the Berne Copyright Convention (1971). No part of this book may be reproduced
or transmitted in any form or by any means, electronic or mechanical, including photocopying, recording, or by any
information storage and retrieval system without permission in writing from the publisher.
We acknowledge the financial support of the Government of Canada through the Book Publishing
Industry Development Program for our publishing activities.
Published by Collector's Guide Publishing Inc., Box 62034, Burlington, Ontario, Canada, L7R 4K2
Printed and bound in Canada
A Shot of Poison / Christopher Long
© 2010 CG Publishing Inc/Christopher Long ISBN 9781-926592-19-0

A SHOT OF
POISON

An Insider's Tales Of One Of Rock's Most Outrageous Bands

Christopher Long

Dedication

To my father and mother — Charles and Barbara Long. If I only knew then what I know now, I would have listened to them — stayed in school and gotten a "real" job. In the end, I gambled my life on rock and roll and all I got was this lousy book!

Editor: C.K. Lendt

Cover concept: Jesse Long
Cover design: JordanDesignStudio.com
Front cover studio photo: Kevin Roberts
Front cover concert photos: Evan Taylor Roach, Christine Herb
Back cover concert photos: Christine Herb, Sandy Creamer
About the Author photo: Kevin Roberts
Front cover model: Katty Pleasant
Ms. Pleasant's make-up: Tia Devine

Acknowledgments

C.K. Lendt, Linda Konner, Rob Godwin, Jesse Long, Bobby Dall, C.C. DeVille, Rikki Rockett, Bret Michaels, Gail Worley, Ian Koss, Jen Cray, Heike Clarke, Chris Dillon, Brad McMahen, Dave Madsen, Karen Madsen, David Thornquest, Melanie Boland, Riki Valentine, Amber Curtis, Scotty Ludwick, Craig Gass, Lisa Dick, The Rook Family, Katty Pleasant, Deana Lane, Barbara Pinnick, Kristen Pinnick, Taylor Stallings, Joe Cantaffa, C.C. Banana, Don Was, Kevin Carter, Tricia White, John Curran, Cathy Pullara, Tom Willett, Christine Herb.

Table of Contents

Foreword

A drummer friend of mine named Brian recently called me from Los Angeles to tell me a very funny story. Back in the early 1990s, he was friendly with members of an up-and-coming rock and roll Hair Band called Desperado. The guys in Desperado were also friends of Poison guitarist C.C. Deville and somehow, through a member of Poison's road crew, they acquired a number of Poison's discarded road cases for use by their own band. For clarification purposes, a "road case" is a hardshell box specifically built to protect musical instruments, audio and lighting production equipment, and other sensitive property when it must be moved between locations and subject to frequent abuse by airport baggage-handlers.

"There were four huge rolling cases," Brian remembered, "and then maybe five or six wardrobe cases, too. I saw them lined up and they took up a good portion of the backyard." When opened, everyone was shocked to discover the cases were still completely packed...with make-up. "It was a ridiculous amount of make-up," Brian recalled with great enthusiasm. "Tons of lipstick! It was incredible!" I asked Brian if it were possible the make-up was merely piled atop something else taking up the bulk of room in the cases, but he said that was unlikely. "They might have used the lower compartments for other things," he surmised, "but I can't imagine them mixing music gear or anything else with their make-up and costumes."

I love this story for the way it so perfectly juxtaposes one prevailing opinion of Poison as the World's Luckiest Marginally Talented Glam Band with another viewpoint that Poison must surely possess ass-loads of ridiculous musical talent if their degree of success affords them the luxury of traveling with eight or nine massive road cases dedicated exclusively to holding their make-up. Love them or hate them, Poison has been a fixture on the music scene for twenty-five years. Making music still pays their bills. And being able to claim the dubious honor of having written and recorded "Unskinny Bop" still gets them laid.

Like *A Shot of Poison* author Christopher Long, I'm a huge fan of the

1980s metal music scene. With a decades-long career as a rock critic for dozens of publications, Chris and I met when he and his partner managed a very talented female singer/songwriter, and they hired me to write a bio for the young artist. With our shameless shared passion for what we affectionately refer to as Hair Metal, Chris and I quickly bonded. My experiences with the band Poison are limited to attendance at perhaps a dozen live shows – some of which I was merely a spectator in the crowd, and others that I attended as a working journalist with the coveted All-Access laminate. I've conducted several interviews with drummer Rikki Rockett for various publications including *Modern Drummer*, but my interactions with the band's other members, vocalist Bret Michaels, guitarist C.C. DeVille and bassist Bobby Dall have been confined to handshakes and head nods. Chris, on the other hand, started out as a fan of Poison's music, later became a friend to individual band members and eventually was hired as part of the group's professional touring entourage. I've only seen the shiny, happy side of Poison. Chris has experienced the seamy underbelly of the Poison beast. As he willingly confesses, much of it is not very pretty.

Chris's eye-opening journey plays out a bit like a rock and roll version of *The Devil Wears Prada*, which is the story of a naïve but ambitious young girl who gets her dream job working as the assistant to the editor of the world's most famous fashion magazine. She hopes this job will be a stepping stone to a writing career. But her boss turns out to be a sadistic, psychotic, egomaniacal taskmaster who tortures her to ill health and near madness. I don't want to toss out any spoilers, but if you know Lauren Weisberger's daunting novel, page through the real-life horror stories so finely elucidated in *A Shot of Poison* and tell me a certain band member doesn't seriously remind you of fictional fashion editor Miranda Priestly. I know, scary.

Chris Long's cautionary tale of life on the road with Poison fully embodies a "Be careful what you wish for, because you just might get it" scenario. But this engaging page-turner also called to mind words spoken to me years ago by my close friend and mentor, veteran heavy metal journalist Vincent Cecolini: "Be wary about meeting your rock heroes," Vinny once advised me. "Sometimes they turn out to be human, and sometimes less than that."

Gail Worley
Modern Drummer Magazine / Worleygig.com
September 2009

Preface

A writer friend of mine once told me that I have a passion for rock and roll. No truer words have been spoken. Most of us who share that passion equate our first rock and roll experience with our first sexual encounter.

It was Christmas 1971 when I was first bitten by the rock and roll bug. My sister Debbie gave me a life altering seven inch single of "Family Affair" by Sly and the Family Stone. Although I was only nine years old, that record blew me away. It was raw, edgy and gritty. It sounded nothing like anything I'd heard on my Partridge Family albums. In fact, it stunk from the funk!

While living in Springfield, Missouri, I celebrated my twelfth birthday in December 1974. It was there that my buddy Brad Pitt (yes, THE Brad Pitt) gave me my first Elton John record. It was a seven inch single of "The Bitch is Back." Thus, I became a diehard Elton fan — that is, until November 1975 when my cousin Cathy turned me onto an amazing new group called Kiss.

By 1976, my teenage obsession with rock music began to concern my extremely conservative parents, Chuck and Barb. As my younger brother Greg and I amassed a huge collection of Kiss 8-track tapes next to the family hi-fi, they became convinced that Gene Simmons was the Devil and that he *and* his followers were all headed straight to Hell.

While attending Stonewall Jackson Junior High School in Orlando, Florida my peers frequented rock concerts. They saw the shows of icons like Kiss, Peter Frampton, Bad Company, Alice Cooper, and Black Sabbath. Meanwhile, because of my parents' restrictions, I settled for second-hand accounts of these often infamous performances the following day at school.

My parents' primary objection to me attending rock concerts was their perception of people freely taking drugs and openly engaging in sexual activities at these events. I thought that was ridiculous. Besides, what did my parents know anyway? At that time they were in their thirties, thus rendering them completely uncool and really old! But when I finally got to attend my first actual rock concert (The Beach Boys) in January 1977, I was amazed by my discovery. Throngs of tie-dyed clad hippies scattered throughout the civic center in Lakeland, Florida — freely smoking dope and openly groping each other. "Holy cow," I said to myself. "My parents were right!"

By the early 1980s I was playing drums in various East Coast Florida bands and attending concerts regularly. From Kiss and Van Halen to Ted Nugent and Aerosmith, I was a constant fixture on the Central Florida concert scene.

By the late 1980s I was fronting my own band, the outrageous, award-winning hard rock act Dead Serios. We performed with such popular bands of the day as Anthrax, Faith No More and Ace Frehley. Considered by some insiders to be "the next big thing," Dead Serios was performing nationwide by 1990, written-up in magazines like *Billboard* and *Creem*. It seemed we were destined for greatness — that is until the Seattle grunge movement became fashionable in 1991 — bringing my show business momentum to a screeching halt.

These are just a few of the many awards I won during the pre-grunge Dead Serios glory days.

Throughout my life, my favorite books have been rock and roll biographies. Before I was old enough to attend an Alice Cooper concert, *Chicago Tribune* columnist Bob Greene had already schooled me in all things Alice in the pages of his 1975 best-seller, *Billion*

Dollar Baby. My interest in rock and roll books continued into my adult life as I devoured such personal favorites as *Neon Angel*, the 1990 autobiography by Runaways singer Cherie Currie and *Kiss and Sell*, the 1997 behind-the-scenes tell-all by former Kiss business manager C.K. Lendt.

Although I've personally never been much of a reader, I was always fascinated with rock biographies.

With my own personal rock and roll dream dashed, I turned to writing in the late 1990s. I began interviewing members of many of my favorite bands like Poison, Cinderella, The Runaways, Quiet Riot and Faster Pussycat. By the early 2000s my monthly columns were read online and in various print publications. One of my most surreal journalistic experiences occurred in 2002 when Poison frontman Bret Michaels called my house to ask for Winger frontman Kip Winger's home phone number. The craziest part was, I actually had the number to give him.

I was somewhat taken aback during the writing of this book when a close friend asked why I was going to "trash" Poison. "Trashing" Poison is the least of my intentions. Poison offered me an opportunity to live out my dream. They brought me into their world and allowed me to experience first-hand life in the rock and roll big league. Some of my experiences with the band were amazing. Some of them sucked. However, I would be doing a disservice to the band, the reader and myself if I were anything less than honest. My point of view in this book is neither pro nor con. I'm merely recounting my personal experiences as they occurred. Besides, at the end of the day, is anybody really going to be interested in, or even believe a collection of sugar-coated, feel good stories regarding a band that has touted itself for nearly twenty-five years as "The Glam Slam Kings of

Noise?" I don't either. I may expose a few intra-band "warts" along the way, but I'm certainly not "trashing" anybody.

I established myself within Poison's inner sanctum many years ago — first as a personal friend of Bobby Dall's, then as a writer — interviewing band members for various print features. Later, as a paid member of their staff, I continued carrying a pocket notebook — writing down everything I saw and heard. In fact, I have mentioned the possibility of a book project to Poison members, their assistants and management staff several times over the years. In 2002 I was hired by the band to write their official press release and in 2006 I was asked to write a bio for Bret Michaels. Consequently, this book should come as no surprise to anyone within the Poison organization.

Me and Rikki Rockett together in Nashville during the 2004 tour.

From being physically threatened by Gene Simmons in 1983 to meeting the members of Aerosmith in 2006, I've had some amazing rock and roll experiences over the years. I discovered early in life that people had great interest in hearing my various insider stories. Even the responses to my behind-the-scenes online blogs are overwhelming. When I returned home from working the 2006 Poison tour, a small hometown party was held in my honor. For hours I was surrounded by close friends, eager to hear my scandalous first- hand accounts of life on the road. I see *A Shot of Poison* simply as a means of sharing my personal rock and roll experiences with an even wider audience of rock and roll friends.

Me with Twisted Sister frontman Dee Snider (Orlando, FL 1997) (top left)

Me and my "ex" Trish with Kiss founder Paul Stanley (Daytona Beach, FL 1992) (above)

Me with rock legend George Thorogood (LA 2000) (left)

I continue to have the utmost admiration for Poison and their tremendous success. Bobby Dall, in particular, has taken me places I would have never been and opened professional doors for me that would have otherwise remained shut. And to this day they remain one of my all-time favorite bands.

Me with a special friend in 2009.
(Photo by Kevin Roberts)

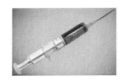

CHAPTER ONE

I WANT ACTION - The early years

In an odd and roundabout way, my Poison connection actually dates back to the late 1970s when I spent my teens living a few miles away from where Bobby Dall lived, who would later become one of the band's founding members. Bobby and I both spent the majority of our youth growing up on Florida's East Coast near the city of Melbourne before he relocated with his family to Pennsylvania in his late teens. We were both budding musicians. We shared many of the same interests, attended the same concerts, hung out with the same crowd and likely bought dope from the same local dealers. However, our paths wouldn't actually cross until adulthood. It was then, in the late 1980s, that I was introduced to the sex, drugs and wild rock and roll world of Poison as the band became an international phenomenon.

The Poison story began with four young musicians from Harrisburg, Pennsylvania — bassist Bobby Dall (Robert Kuykendall, born November 2, 1963), drummer Rikki Rockett (Richard Ream, born August 8, 1961), guitarist Matt Smith, and lead vocalist Bret Michaels (Bret Michael Sychak, born March 15, 1963 — named after the character, Bret Maverick, from the TV series, *Maverick* that began in the late 1950s.). They came together in pursuit of their rock and roll dream. The year was 1983 and the pop charts were owned by such polished, squeaky-clean artists as Michael Jackson, Rick Springfield and Huey Lewis. Inspired by the outrageous, androgynous look and raw, punk sound of such early 1970s glam rock icons as Alice Cooper, T. Rex and the New York Dolls, these long-haired upstarts had little interest in contributing to the musical status quo. They were determined to be different, to be noticed, and to take over the world or die trying. By 1984 they recognized they would have to leave their humdrum hometown if they were to stand even a remote chance of succeeding. New York and Los Angeles then presented the best opportunities for aspiring new bands. Lured by its warm and sunny climate, the boys from Harrisburg chose to relocate in California. With little more than pocket change, some eye-liner and sheer determination, they headed west. Soon, the members of the band, known at that time as Paris, found themselves struggling to survive while paying their dues on LA's cut-throat club scene.

FIRST AREA APPEARANCE

RAINBOW SKATING ARENA
CARLISLE PIKE, MECH.

OCTOBER 21st
10:00 TO 1:00

SPECIAL GUEST BAND

SEARGANT ROCK AND THE COMMANDOES

TICKETS AVAILABLE AT DOOR

In need of a stronger name, Paris would soon become Poison.

Shortly after arriving in LA, the band briefly stayed at the home of music producer and songwriter Kim Fowley. Over the years, Fowley had become successful as the producer of many artists including The Runaways and Warren Zevon. He also co-wrote songs with Alice Cooper, Kiss and other top-name rock acts. Uncomfortable with his

An early Poison show flyer prior to Matt's departure.

eccentricities (e.g., shaving his cat for fun), Bret, Rikki and Matt didn't stay long at Fowley's. However, recognizing Fowley's brilliance, Bobby stuck around — eager to learn from the industry vet's experiences. During his stay, Fowley suggested the band come up with a stronger name — one better suited for developing an outrageous image. The band decided on Poison.

Weary of their lean existence, Matt returned to Pennsylvania and after numerous auditions was replaced by Brooklyn native C.C. DeVille (Bruce Anthony Johannesson, born May 14, 1962).

C.C. had also been struggling to find his niche on the LA scene. It has been rumored that prior to auditioning for Poison, C.C. had been a member of Roxx Regime — an early version of the Christian glam band Stryper. But, in 2009 a Stryper source informed me that although C.C. had briefly rehearsed with Roxx Regime, he never wrote, recorded or performed with the religious rockers.

Heavily influenced by the pop songwriting of Cheap Trick, C.C. offered Poison some of *his* songs.

"Cheap Trick are my 'Beatles'."

C.C. DeVille, June 2006

Poison's classic lineup was in place. They also had a bold new name to match their striking, New York Dolls-inspired glam look. Combining such onstage visuals as smoke, trash cans and garbage with over-the-top, high-energy, cock-rock swagger, Poison was becoming THE "must see" band on LA's club scene. They were selling-out such legendary venues as The Whisky a Go Go, The Troubadour and The Country Club, yet major record labels still turned a deaf ear to Poison. Their fortunes were about to change, however, now that C.C.'s catchy melodies and hook-laden guitar riffs were at the core of their music.

Poison signed with Enigma Records, a California-based independent label in 1986. On a shoestring budget of $30,000 the band recorded their debut album, *Look What the Cat Dragged In*, produced by Ric Browde in less than two weeks. The album cover featured pictures of the band members looking more like hot chicks than rockin' dudes and has been described as a glam version of The Beatles' 1970 *Let it Be* cover. In his review of *Look What the Cat Dragged In* for the *Rolling Stone Album Guide*, critic Rob Sheffield commented that Poison, "looked like four slices of wedding cake that escaped out of the bakery window." The record sold 40,000 units as an independent release in the summer of 1986. Poison was now on the road, struggling on the US club circuit. Enigma soon merged with industry giant Capitol Records and with the newfound benefit of major label distribution and resources, "Talk Dirty to Me" became a surprise Top Ten hit in early 1987. After years of hard work, Poison had become another "overnight" success on the national rock and roll scene.

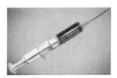

I worked at The Tape Deck Music Center in Melbourne throughout the 1980s. From records, cassettes and 8-track tapes to posters, T-shirts, and smoking paraphernalia, The Tape Deck was a classic, old school record shop. I recall when *Look What the Cat Dragged In* hit stores in 1986. Initially, I was hardly a Poison fan. Although I followed many of the top rock bands of the day such as Van Halen, AC/DC, Kiss and Mötley Crüe, many of my favorite musical artists at that time were classic R&B acts like Rufus, Lakeside, Shalamar and Ohio Players. I perceived Poison's extreme androgynous, glam image as ridiculous and completely excessive — even for my liberal artistic taste. And to me, "Talk Dirty to Me" was simply a shameful rip off of Cheap Trick's 1982 hit "She's Tight." However, after being forced by my friend and co-worker Brad McMahen to endure their debut record repeatedly at work, throughout 1986 and 1987, I could no longer resist Poison's catchy pop metal sound.

The reaction women had toward Poison was immediate and intense. The Tape Deck was also a Ticketmaster outlet so I remember when Poison came through Florida in the spring of 1987 as an opening act for Ratt. Few ticket buyers whom I serviced seemed to have much interest in the headliner. However, from teenage girls to older married women, Melbourne's female rockers were losing their minds over the outrageous Poison and their bad-boy mystique. I remember girls coming into my shop and buying tickets for the Jacksonville show. The day after, they'd be back for tickets to that night's Orlando show. Then I'd see them the next day buying tickets for the Tampa show. One of my frequent customers, a female corrections officer, actually took a week-long leave of absence from her job in order to follow Poison from town to town.

It was during the summer of 1987 when I first became aware of a possible personal connection to Poison. One of my co-workers at The Tape Deck was a beautiful, petite brunette in her early twenties named Jackie Rook. About the time that Poison's hit single, "I Won't Forget You" was hitting the MTV airwaves, Jackie mentioned to me at work that she had grown up with the group's bass player. Initially, I thought she was full of shit. I had known Jackie and her brothers for years and I didn't recall them hanging out with anyone who looked like Bobby Dall. A few days later Jackie came to work with a photo of herself taken five years earlier at an Allman Brothers Band concert with a kid who she claimed was Bobby. Skinny as a rail and looking like what I can only describe as a pothead-hippie, I was skeptical that the punk in the photo was the glam rock musician I had been seeing on TV. However, I became a believer once I saw photos of Jackie and her family hanging out backstage with Bobby in 1988.

Bobby Dall backstage (seated middle) with our longtime
friends, the Rook family in 1988.
(Photo courtesy of Monique Rook)

Poison flaunted their early success by airbrushing their
second album cover on the back of their 1988 tour bus.
(Photo courtesy of Monique Rook)

The first time I saw Poison live was October 1988. Although I had finally become a fan, I primarily went to the concert to see opening act, Lita Ford. At that point, Poison had just become headliners. "Every Rose Has its Thorn" was a radio hit and the concert was a sell-out. In fact, I had never seen such a large crowd at Daytona's Ocean Center. This was back in the days before all concerts had assigned seating. I had gotten stuck in traffic on my way to the show so I wound up sitting in the back of the 10,000 seat venue's upper deck. Despite the hype over Poison being such an amazing live act, I found them to be sloppy. The sound sucked and I went home feeling disappointed.

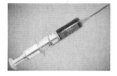

By the late 1980s Bret, Rikki and C.C. were living the rock star lifestyle in LA's fast lane. However, Bobby chose to escape the Hollywood scene and returned to his quiet Florida hometown of Melbourne.

In their early days, Poison employed as an assistant, Riki "R.V." Valentine. R.V. was a true rock and roll jack-of-all-trades. He was

part roadie, part hairdresser and part bodyguard rolled into one dysfunctional yet loveable mess. One of R.V.'s more tantalizing duties while touring with Poison during the 1980s was to procure girls for the band's nightly after-show parties. Shunning the term "pimp," R.V. preferred the title "Entertainment Director." While off tour he would typically reside at Bobby's new house in Melbourne. After a while R.V. began living at other places in the Melbourne area, often sharing apartments or trailers with various strippers and other wayward young females.

Longtime Poison associate Riki
"R.V" Valentine in 1990.
(Photo by Ramon Scavelli)

Before long, R.V. became a regular fixture on Melbourne's local rock club scene. He frequented the Power Station nightclub where my band Dead Serios often performed. We became fast friends and

in 1990 he began dating my good friend Melanie Boland. Melanie was a beautiful seventeen-year-old part-time model and student who frequented The Tape Deck. She was also a regular on the local rock scene and a dedicated Dead Serios fan. As their relationship developed, Melanie would share stories with me about hanging out with R.V. and the members of Poison. As an up-and-coming performer, I enjoyed hearing Melanie's insider rock and roll tales. I was especially thrilled when she invited Bobby

Dead Serios in the early 1990s.
(Photo by Ramon Scavelli)

R.V. and I headed home from a 1991 Dead Serios gig. Photo by Lisa Alteri)

Dall and myself to attend her eighteenth birthday dinner party at her parents' Melbourne home in July 1990.

Bobby was now an established rock star. *Look What the Cat Dragged In* reached #3 on the *Billboard* charts and sold over three million units. Their sophomore release, *Open Up and Say... Ahh!*, peaked at #2 on *Billboard* in 1988 and sold five million-plus units. In the summer of 1990 Poison's third record, *Flesh and Blood* was released. It shipped platinum. The record also peaked at #2 and sold in excess of three million units. Within a matter of three years Poison had evolved from the depths of LA's club scene to becoming a nationwide sensation. By incorporating a flair for rock fashion with androgynous make- up and sky-high hair styles, Poison defined the 1980s Hair Band genre. Their outlandish and colorful visual persona helped make them the darlings of MTV, boasting popular, high energy music videos for such hits as "Talk Dirty to Me," "I Want Action," "I Won't Forget You," "Nothin' But a Good Time," "Fallen Angel," "Something to Believe In," "Unskinny Bop," and the #1 single, "Every Rose Has its Thorn."

My friend Melanie Boland introduced me to Bobby Dall during the band's hey day. (Photo by Jennifer Boland)

CHAPTER ONE

Although Poison's look was outrageous, they were hardly threatening. In fact, in a February 1989 concert review, *New York Times* critic Peter Watrous referred to Poison's image as "a cartoon version of decadence."

Not being one to miss a promotional opportunity and desperate for my own show business break, I arrived at Melanie's party with a Dead Serios demo tape ready to deliver to her "A" list guest. Though I had been friends with R.V. for about a year, this was my first experience meeting Bobby face-to-face, so I arrived prepared. Bobby is one of the most honest and direct, no-bullshit type of guys on the planet. Early in our conversation Bobby expressed his extreme dislike for receiving demo tapes. Disappointed and a little embarrassed, my demo remained in my pocket.

Melanie's birthday bash turned out to be a small, casual dinner party. In fact, the guest list only included five people: Bobby and his wife Michelle, me and my wife Trish, and of course, R.V. I was nervous about meeting Bobby for the first time, however, he was very cool and easy-going. At dinner I remember him leaning over and whispering to me about how he hated the chicken entrée Melanie's mother had served that night. This led him to offering me suggestions for lyrics to a song that I was writing coincidentally called "Tastes Like Chicken." Overall, everybody had a good time that night, hanging out on the porch telling stories and cracking jokes into the evening. Upon my departure that night I thought to myself, "Screw it! This might be my only shot." So I slid Bobby my demo on my way out the door. Although he graciously accepted my cassette, Dead Serios's hardcore style was the antithesis of Poison's polished, arena rock sound. Consequently, Bobby had no interest in Dead Serios, despite being at the forefront of Florida's new music scene.

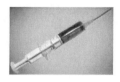

The first time I was invited to Bobby's house I was in drop-jaw amazement. The first thing I noticed was that Bobby had a swimming pool in his *front* yard. It just so happened that on that particular summer day in 1990 the pool was filled with several bikini-clad babes. I remember thinking that was pretty cool. Additionally, the walls inside Bobby's home were covered with gold and platinum records, photos and awards documenting his undeniable rock star status. For an aspiring young musician like myself, that visit made a lasting impression.

R.V. promised Bobby that he'd have a large piece of recording gear shipped to LA via the Melbourne airport. I owned a Dodge Rampage (mini) pick-up truck and thus was deployed to help transport the equipment from Bobby's to the airport.

During one of my first visits to his house I got to experience first-hand the blunt, no-bullshit side of Bobby I mentioned earlier. It was the day before he left town to kick off the *Flesh and Blood* tour. I was sitting on the couch in his living room, admiring his prominently displayed memorabilia as he spoke to a fellow band member on the phone.

"Fuck him!" Bobby shouted into the telephone receiver. "He's not the only star in this band. Who the fuck does he think he is?" Although it wasn't my place to ask who he was talking to or who he was talking about, I could wager a guess. And let's just say, expletives aside, that Bobby's blunt and direct tone conveyed his honest opinions to the band member he was ranting to on the phone.

Later that afternoon we sat outside Bobby's house while part-time hair stylist R.V. gave him a pre-tour trim. In the midst of our conversation Bobby commented to me, "If you've got problems in your band before you get signed, they'll only get worse after you get a platinum record." He would certainly prove to be right about that.

"If you've got problems in your band before you get signed, they'll only get worse after you get a platinum record."

Bobby Dall, July 1990

Each of Poison's first three albums were Top Ten multi-million-sellers.

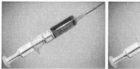 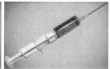

CHAPTER TWO

SOULS ON FIRE - *Crashing and burning in the '90s*

Poison was a rock powerhouse in the summer of 1990. *Flesh and Blood* was quickly on its way to becoming their third consecutive multi-million-selling record. But as their fame reached new heights, I noticed cracks in the band's platinum foundation.

While on break from the *Flesh and Blood* tour Poison members spent significant time at Bobby's place in Florida. They slept by day, but by night the Poison boys were becoming notorious troublemakers on Melbourne's late night club scene and things were starting to get ugly. Employees *and* patrons of after-hours establishments like Last Call and The Producers all seemed to have their own wild Poison stories. These tales typically involved various band members and tag-alongs all with the "sniffles" who were jammed into bathroom stalls at various Melbourne clubs during late night hours. Poison members were shamelessly flaunting their self-indulgent rock star lifestyles. To add insult to injury, they were starting to get sloppy and careless in their public behavior. Their negligence had not gone unnoticed.

One night in particular, Bobby, C.C. and part of the band's entourage showed up at The Power Station nightclub where I was performing. They were loud, shit-faced and indiscrete about their public presence. I was in the back office of the club going over some business with the owners, Jeff and Greg Kimple, when C.C. came barging in. He was wired and extremely rude. For some reason he felt compelled to share very graphic details of an alleged anal sex experience he had with a popular young female pop star of that day.

During Poison's heyday, they appeared regularly on the covers of rock's top magazines.

Although C.C. and I would later become friends, my first impression was that he was an unlikable and obnoxious jerk.

That night, about fifteen minutes before closing time somebody called for an impromptu "last call" jam session. After being dug out of an over-crowded men's room stall, Bobby and C.C. wiped their noses and joined me and Dead Serios drummer Bill Erwin on stage.

By this time, Bobby was so shit-faced that he could barely *hold* a bass, let alone *play* one. So an annoyed, yet equally fucked up C.C. made Bobby sit back in the audience while a local and more sober bass player from the crowd was brought onstage to join in on what had to be one of the all-time worst versions of Led Zeppelin's "Rock and Roll." For starters, as a vocalist I have no business trying to recreate any Robert Plant tunes, and secondly, C.C. was so wasted that he couldn't (or wouldn't) wrap up his own guitar solo and end the musical nightmare. It was verging on ridiculous. It was now closing time and club security had turned on all of the house lights and yet C.C. just kept extending his solo. When I *tried* to come back in with the vocal, C.C. literally kicked me in the ass right on stage and kept playing. So I just let him "hang himself" and somehow we eventually managed to get out of it. Oddly enough, the crowd loved it!

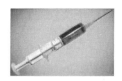

By the time their *Flesh and Blood* tour rolled into Orlando, Florida on March 24, 1991 Poison's infamous live show had taken a noticeable back seat to the after-show party. The band appeared to be spinning out of control. At this point Bobby and I were established friends and I looked forward to seeing him backstage that night after the concert.

For those not familiar with the backstage after-show scene, let me say that unless you're a stripper or a dope dealer, the experience is not quite as glamorous as you may expect. More often than not, an after-show party involves dozens of business associates, family, friends and a few lucky fans of the band being herded like cattle and crammed into a backstage holding cell (usually an empty catering room) by venue or band security. Typically there are barely enough complimentary beverages at these "parties" to accommodate even a handful of guests. In fact, the experience is often so uncomfortable that years later while working as a personal assistant with Poison, I was frequently offered money by hot, thirsty after-show guests to bring them additional bottled water or soft drinks from a dressing room or tour bus.

In the meantime, band members typically return to their dressing rooms to shower, change into fresh clothes and relax for a few minutes while enjoying a late night meal prior to meeting their after-show guests. Frequently they take time to discuss various issues from that evening's show with other band and production staff members. And *sometimes* they get sidetracked by various extracurricular backstage activities. Unfortunately, due to these behind-the-scenes distractions, after-show guests are often kept waiting for their rock and roll heroes for an hour or more, only to be turned away with nothing more than a glimpse of a road manager or personal assistant announcing that "the band will not be coming down tonight."

For better or worse, on this particular night at Orlando's O-Rena, Bobby did make an after-show appearance. I greeted him at the backstage hospitality room door and I was shocked to discover that he was more impaired than I had ever seen him before. Although he once told me that he was "never too fucked-up to perform," he had-

31

n't been off the stage terribly long when I saw him that night and believe me, the guy was pretty "fucked- up." Grinding his jaw, he leaned toward me and whispered in my ear, "Walk with me. Walk with me." I looked him in the eye and saw the embodiment of the expression, "the lights were on but nobody was home." It was obvious that my buddy was too wasted to walk or even stand on his own.

"I was never too fucked up to perform."
Bobby Dall, May 2006

So I took him by the arm and led him around the room to greet his adoring fans. I was a bit freaked out because the guy could barely speak and there was nothing that I could do to help him. Before long, R.V. came to rescue Bobby from the meet-and-greet and safely loaded him on the tour bus. But by now it was becoming much too obvious that Bobby's lifestyle was completely kicking his ass.

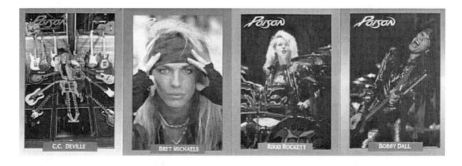

At the height of their popularity Poison was included in a series of rock and roll trading cards.

The excesses of fame were becoming uncontrollable for Poison by the early 1990s, yet some of their darkest moments would ultimately help to immortalize the band and their "bad boy" reputation. Although Bobby would later laugh about it, many found Poison's appearance at MTV's 1991 *Video Music Awards* show to be an embarrassing disaster. Although I thought C.C.'s flaming, hot pink hair color that night was amazing, even I couldn't deny their appalling musical performance. To amplify Poison's problems, it was presented on live television. The band was now imploding in front of the entire world.

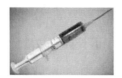

Barely reaching the Top Fifty, 1991's *Swallow This* marked the end of Poison's platinum streak.

Their next album, *Swallow This, Live* was released in the fall of 1991 and barely reached the *Billboard* Top Fifty. Conflicts between Bret and C.C., primarily for musical control of the band, were getting physical and before long C.C. was fired from Poison.

1993's *Native Tongue* was recorded with C.C.'s replacement, renowned guitar ace Richie Kotzen. Although the record did crack the *Billboard* Top Twenty, ultimately achieving gold status, it

Poison's gold 1993 *Native Tongue* would be their last studio record for seven years.

seemed that Poison's "fifteen minutes" were running out. After an affair was discovered between Richie and Rikki's girlfriend, Richie was also fired from the band and replaced by Blues Saraceno.

The band remained busy during 1994 working on material for their next record, *Crack a Smile* at Bobby's house in Florida. Rikki told me how much he enjoyed making *Crack a Smile* because there was no record label pressure. With the added edge of Saraceno's guitar work they were able to create a record on their own terms. In 1995 I can remember R.V. playing demo tracks from the album while I was in LA. I was struck with how fresh and exciting the new songs sounded. Unfortunately having no pressure from the label was not entirely a positive situation. Capitol Records had lost interest in Poison and ultimately shelved *Crack a Smile*.

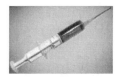

Not unlike many rock acts of their day, Poison had fallen victim to their own excesses, egos and infighting. Like a thief in the night, the music scene had changed as well. There was no place for Poison in the new grunge era that Nirvana ushered in. As early as 1991 Bobby was already indicating to me that he felt burnt out and thought Poison needed a break. The short-lived grunge movement provided them with that hiatus.

"Nirvana was never out to destroy any-body but the dinosaurs and the baby just got thrown out with the bath water on that one." Rikki Rockett, September 2003

Band members embraced their off-time in various ways. C.C. continued making new music with various bands in LA, including a power-pop trio known at the time as The Stepmothers. Rikki kept busy developing his Southern California-based comic book company called No Mercy. On his way home following a wild night of partying at a Hollywood nightclub on May 24, 1994, Bret lost control and crashed his Ferrari. Although he survived the accident, he did sustain a broken nose, broken ribs and lost several teeth. Bret also began a second career in feature films. He formed Sheen/Michaels Entertainment with longtime friend, actor Charlie Sheen, and Bret directed and acted in the films *A Letter From Death Row* and *No Code of Conduct*. Conversely, Bobby chose to all but completely leave the entertainment business and opened Go Dog Go, a drive-thru hot dog restaurant in Palm Bay, Florida. In fact, with his new, extremely close-cropped, "regular-guy" haircut, I almost didn't recognize him when we ran into each other one morning at our local Barnes & Noble store in 1998. But he was still the same ol' Bobby at heart, as he remained focused on my girlfriend's ass while I tried recruiting him in the bookstore coffee shop for a new band I was putting together called The Dadz. Neither his restaurant nor my new band lasted very long.

R.V. examines the wreckage following Bret's near-fatal 1994 car crash.
(Photo courtesy of Riki Valentine)

Without the support of their longtime label, Poison had literally disappeared from the music scene by the mid 1990s. They had no fan club — not even a Web site. It seemed that they were destined to become just another entry in rock's ever-growing "Where are they now?" file. However, with little fanfare, Capitol Records released *Poison's Greatest Hits* in November 1996. At the height of the Hair Band backlash, Poison scored yet another platinum

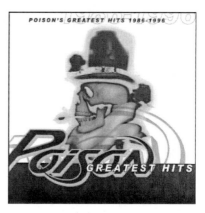

With little fanfare, Poison's *Greatest Hits* became the band's fourth platinum-selling record.

record. For their remaining diehard fans, there was finally a glimmer of hope that reports of Poison's death had indeed been exaggerated.

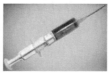 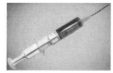

CHAPTER THREE

LOOK WHAT THE CAT DRAGGED IN (Again)

Clean, (somewhat) sober and facing a radically different music scene, the classic Poison lineup reunited in 1999 after an eight year hiatus. And to the disappointment and disbelief of their critics, they came back like gangbusters. With their legendary, high energy stage show and a toned down, not-so-glam look, Poison once again became a major box office attraction.

Poison duplicated the success of their 1999 reunion tour with another summer outing in 2000. Also, proving they were no nostalgia act, Poison had not one, but two new records in stores in 2000. There was such renewed interest in the group that Capitol Records finally released the (almost forgotten) *Crack a Smile* record in the spring. By the summer the band had released *Power to the People* on their own newly formed Cyanide label. The record contained a collection of live recordings of their classic hits combined with five new studio tracks, an album sputnikmusic.com referred to as offering "the worst of both worlds." Also in 2000, C.C. released the debut record from his own band, Samantha 7 (formerly The Stepmothers).

By 2001 Poison's annual fifty-plus city summer tours were outselling those of many newer bands. Performing throughout the decade with other rock and roll heavyweights such as Kiss, Def Leppard, Ratt, Dokken, Cinderella, Warrant and Skid Row, Poison was once again performing to an average of 10,000 fans nightly in arenas and amphitheaters across the country.

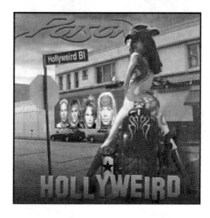

Crack a Smile, Power to the People and *Hollyweird* were Poison's first three post-grunge era records.

There was no doubt that Poison was back in a big way. However, the media was not treating them with the respect they deserved. In the early 2000s, rock critic Scott Reid wrote, "Poison is the least worthwhile rock band to ever hit it big." Consequently, as a rock writer myself, I frequently defended Poison in my monthly music columns which appeared in such Florida entertainment publications as, *Brevard Live*, *Jam* and *The Buzz*.

Although I had been friends with Bobby for many years by the spring of 2001, I hadn't officially interviewed anyone from his band. They were preparing for the upcoming *Glam Slam Metal Jam* summer tour with Warrant, Quiet Riot and Enuff Z'nuff when I

My 2001 Poison cover story in *Brevard Live* took me to the next level within the band's organization.

approached Bobby with the idea of a Poison cover story and interview. It would appear in the June issue of Florida's east coast arts and entertainment magazine, *Brevard Live*. Bobby made it clear that unless the situation required the participation of all four band members (e.g., a VH-1 special) he simply, "did not do press." However, because of our longtime personal relationship he made an exception and agreed to an interview with me.

Although Rikki, Bret, and C.C. had all released solo records in the 2000s, Bobby told me in 2001 that he had "no plans for side projects or solo albums."

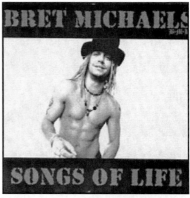

When the June 2001 issue of *Brevard Live* hit the streets both Poison and their management seemed pleased with the feature cover story. In fact, Bobby even called me from the road to express his satisfaction. The following year, I was hired by the band to co-write their official press release with frontman Bret Michaels.

Soon I had graduated within the Poison organization to what Bobby called "laminate status." Consequently, each tour I would be issued an official all-access laminated backstage pass. I could now show up at any Poison concert at any time and pretty much come, go and do as I pleased. Bobby once commented that my all-access passes were "the keys to the kingdom" and warned me not to "fuck it up" or "abuse" the privilege.

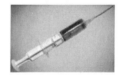

For C.C. and Bobby, the fight to remain sober would be an uphill battle in the 2000s. Although many dark days were still to come, life on the road with Poison after the 1999 reunion was often more funny than frightening. For instance, I was with Bobby at his personal after-show meet-and-greet at Cleveland, Ohio's Blossom Music Center in July 2001. All of a sudden, we heard a helluva commotion coming from down the hall. Without warning the door to the hospitality room burst open and in walked C.C. in all of his bombastic glory. He was clanging bells, hollering like a lunatic and wearing a sandwich board sign that read "Kisses for a Dollar!" Even at someone else's gathering, C.C. is still the life of the party.

"C.C. DeVille is one of my dearest friends in the world. I laugh my ass off at him day in and day out."

Bobby Dall, April 2001

This warm and fuzzy photo of me with Bobby and his son Zak was taken backstage on July 19, 2001 at The Blossom Music Center in Cleveland, Ohio.

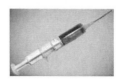

Unfortunately the 2001 tour came to an abrupt end in August when Bobby had to undergo emergency neck surgery to remedy a condition that had plagued him since his youth. In 2001 it was further aggravated during a go-cart accident while on tour. Although Poison's Web site was full of photos from the actual surgery, several individuals commented on various other Web sites that Bobby's neck was a convenient excuse to prematurely end the tour either because

of poor ticket sales or because Poison could no longer handle being blown away each night by opening act Quiet Riot. As a witness to at least a dozen dates on that tour who was in regular contact with Bobby, I can assure all cyber-geeks that these assertions were completely erroneous.

Me and Mr. Rockett together on July 29, 2001 at Nashville's AM South Amphitheater.

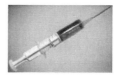

While covering Poison's 2002 *Hollyweird* tour for *Brevard Live*, I discovered that Rikki and I shared a passion for Quisp breakfast cereal. The Quisp character is a cute fluorescent green and purple space alien. The cereal is shaped like flying saucers and tastes like Cap'n Crunch. We both loved the cereal as little kids in the 1960s before it was taken off the market around 1970. Coincidentally, early in the 2000s Quaker Oats had brought Quisp back as a specialty item that was only available online and in a select few grocery store chains.

I thought I'd surprise Rikki by bringing him a case of the tasty treat backstage at Poison's May 27 show in Nashville. This was a few months after the September 11, 2001 terrorist attack on the World Trade Center and security was tight everywhere. I needed to

get the package to Rikki but at the time I wasn't really familiar with the backstage layout of the AM South Amphitheater so I asked a friendly member of the venue's security staff for a little assistance. Within seconds, I found myself sitting in the venue's executive office being questioned by people with walkie talkies. They wanted to know who *I* was, who *Rikki Rockett* was, where I was going, what I was doing and exactly what was in *that* package!

Although some folks are "Coo-Coo" for Cocoa Puffs, Rikki Rockett and I are "Quazy" for Quisp!

"It's just breakfast cereal," I told the men in suits who had gathered around me. However, with my hair dyed pink, multiple piercings and tattoos, I wasn't exactly perceived as credible. And as soon as they realized that Rikki was a member of Poison, they definitely didn't believe that the package contained just cereal. But for some reason they never bothered to open the package. Finally, after several minutes of backroom debate I was escorted backstage to make my delivery. Rikki was thrilled with my offering, later confessing to me that he, "ate the fuck out of that shit!"

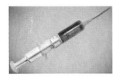

By 2002 I was beginning to interview the members of Poison on a somewhat regular basis. While Bobby is open, frank and painfully honest, I've found frontman Bret Michaels to be more savvy. Always armed with an arsenal of well-rehearsed and very print-friendly quotes, he's a master of self promotion and never fails to give a very calculated interview.

"I really love going out there and playing kick-ass rock and roll. I'm as excited about seeing the fans as they are to see the show."

Bret Michaels, March 2002

"I would play music whether I made it or not."

Bret Michaels, March 2002

LOOK WHAT THE CAT DRAGGED IN (Again)

Poison's LA shows are typically a star-studded affair. From current TV and movie-types like David Spade to rock legends like Carmine Appice to pop culture oddities like Leif Garrett, nearly everybody who is or ever was somebody in Hollywood all turn out when Poison is in town. In fact, in 2002 and 2003 the LA guest list at the Universal Amphitheater was so extensive that VIPs waited an hour or more to get through the line at the Will Call window and into the venue. Unlike other Poison shows I had experienced, the 2002 and 2003 LA after-show parties actually lasted throughout the entire show. From the first chords of the opening act until the final pyro blast of Poison's set, the LA backstage area was full of hip scenesters hanging out, too cool to watch the show from out front.

Backstage in LA (2002) with a special friend and Faster Pussycat frontman Taime Downe.

Backstage in LA (2003) with my ex-fiancé Vicki and Skid Row guitarist Dave "Snake" Sabo. (I went blond for a while. What was I thinking?)

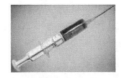

My interviews with Bret have all been pre-tour phoners (telephone interviews) and after about our third phoner we had become comfortable enough with each other that he'd occasionally let his guard down and get real. In 2003 Poison was preparing for the *Louder, Harder, Faster* tour. Bret had recently released his first solo album *Songs of Life* and he was clearly frustrated over trying to get his new single and video on the airwaves in a post-grunge music world.

"There is an absolute prejudice against having a straight up rock video anymore. There is such a fucking wall put up that it makes me sometimes wanna fucking scream!"

Bret Michaels, April 2003

"It's all about payola. It's all about pay-to-play and I refuse to play that game. I just feel sometimes the fact that I've been around for eighteen years should stand on its own. What happened to just being played just because it's a great song?"

Bret Michaels, April 2003

LOOK WHAT THE CAT DRAGGED IN (Again)

In 2003 I approached *Brevard Live* editor Heike Clarke about creating a new column for the magazine. This monthly segment would feature interviews with various nationally known drummers. As a drummer myself, I knew exactly who I wanted to interview for the first edition.

My interview with Rikki was scheduled to take place backstage at Nashville's AM South Amphitheater prior to Poison's concert on September 1. I arrived at the venue on time, promptly at 3PM. While I was waiting on Rikki, Bret and part of the crew organized a football game out behind the now defunct AM South venue. When throwing the ball around at home with my son Jesse, I'm a regular Joe Montana. However, I knew if I accepted the offer to join *this* game I would have made a fool of myself, and I definitely didn't want to look like a pussy in front of these guys! Also, even at my best, I couldn't compete with Bret. He's got a powerful arm and throws with amazing Troy Aikman-like accuracy. So I did my best to appear cool, watching from the sidelines while waiting for Rikki to prepare for the interview.

By 4PM Rikki's dressing room had been cleared of all tour staff and a "Do Not Disturb" sign was posted outside the door. We spent the next hour and a half hanging out — discussing drums, technique, influences, style and chicks while munching on Twizzlers and watching vintage concert footage on his laptop of one of our all-time favorite bands, 1970s glam rockers, Angel. With their outrageous white stage outfits and platform boots, Angel was once referred to as a "good-guy" version of Kiss. Their hard-driving, pop-metal style provided the musical blueprint Poison would follow in later years.

"I met Punky Meadows (Angel) a couple of years ago and he was not a nice man."

Rikki Rockett, September 2003

I typically try to get my interviewees to relax enough to drop their guard and engage in an open and honest dialogue. Sometimes that's easier said than done. In fact, I frequently ask musicians very obvious and dopey questions just to get them talking. My theory is that even on tough interviews, if I can get the artist to talk long enough I can usually at least obtain a few notable quotes. Prompting Rikki to open up was never a problem and he definitely did not let me down.

"I don't know what Joey Kramer (Aerosmith) thinks of me, but I think Joey's God!"

Rikki Rockett, September 2003

At one point during the interview he said to me, "I guess you heard about the fire." Just a couple of nights earlier en route to Detroit, the brake line on one of the eighteen-wheelers transporting Poison's equipment caught fire and the band's entire stage show went up in flames. According to Rikki, only a few guitars and a portion of their lighting gear had been salvaged. Poison, the band known for their wild show and spectacular lighting, hit the stage in Detroit the following night with nothing more than a couple of borrowed amps and a rented drum kit. They didn't even have a drum riser. Rikki added that the review in the local paper the next morning reported that the "stripped down" Poison delivered one of their best shows ever!

"I play hard but I'm not a basher. I'm really just a kick, snare, hi-hat guy, I always have been. I play for the song."

Rikki Rockett, September 2003

During our conversation Rikki told me about one of his current video projects. It was to be a documentary based on his life patterned after VH-1's popular *Behind the Music* series. Realizing that I was a huge fan of his, Rikki was struck with the notion that *he* should interview *me* for his project. Initially I thought he was goofing, but shortly after the concert I was approached by Big John, one of the band's longtime security guys. The intimidating yet lovable six-foot-plus assistant hollered over the backstage ruckus, "Rikki needs you in the dressing room for the interview."

"Punk was never out to destroy glitter rock. It was out to destroy prog (progressive) rock.

Rikki Rockett, September 2003

CHAPTER THREE

Before any video taping began, the group's wardrobe manager Janna Elias came into the dressing room. She was organizing the band members' apparel for a VH-1 special that was slated to tape within the next few days in New York. Rikki took one look at the outfits selected for the show and threw a fit.

The legendary and lovable Big John with my friend Jamie Bass in 2003. (Photo by Amber Curtis)

"We used to be dangerous!" Rikki shouted as he leaped to his feet from his relaxed position lying on the dressing room floor. "Look at this," he commanded with disgust, pointing to a T-shirt hanging from the wardrobe rack. "C.C. has been wearing this same Johnny Cash shirt every night of the tour — and Bobby wears this baseball jersey! A baseball jersey? We used to be cool! And Bret — I don't even know what's going on with him!"

Once Rikki had finally regained his composure he sat me down on a stool in the dressing room and instructed Big John to clip a microphone on my shirt. Standing in a dark corner in the room, smoking a cigarette, and assuming the role of an investigative reporter, Rikki began asking me questions similar to what we had discussed earlier in the day. Unfortunately, soon after the lights and camera went on, any journalistic integrity that I may have possessed flew out the window. I became so self-conscious about trying to be cool in this video that my mind blanked and I'm sure I came off like a real dope. Although I don't think anything ever became of the project, I did get to see some edited footage a few weeks later. My quotes were sandwiched between those of famous rockers and other industry insiders and fortunately (thanks to some great editing) I only came off like a half dip-shit.

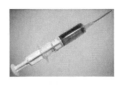

LOOK WHAT THE CAT DRAGGED IN (Again)

About an hour prior to Poison taking the Nashville stage in 2003, I headed down a backstage corridor on my way to Bobby's dressing room. At that moment the scene was relatively quiet when suddenly, a half-naked Skid Row guitarist Dave "Snake" Sabo stumbled out of his band's dressing room, into the hallway. Serving as one of the opening acts on the tour, it appeared that Sabo and his colleagues were enjoying an after-show celebration. Earlier that day, Skid Row

guitarist Scotty Hill had invited me to "hang out" with his band that night. He even offered to do an interview with me. Despite his generous proposal, I didn't think it was my place to intrude upon what appeared to be a private shindig. However, since Sabo had conveniently left the dressing room door wide open, I saw no harm in sneaking a peek at the festivities.

Skid Row's wildman Scotty Hill live onstage.
(Photo by Christine Herb)

As I walked past the open door, it appeared their dressing room had been transformed into a kind of psychedelic rock and roll/disco strip club. Colored lights flashed and twirled as girls danced to music blasting in the background. The scene was reminiscent of a 1970s porno flick. Even after the departure of charismatic original frontman Sebastian Bach, it was still (monkey) business as usual for the Skid Row boys. In hindsight, maybe I should have joined in after all.

Rikki Rockett sharing a "broke back" moment with Skid Row drummer Phil Varone in Illinois on September 7, 2003. (Photo by Jamie Bass)

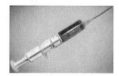

In stark contrast to the wild Skid Row gala down the hall, the vibe in Bobby's dressing room was more like a faculty lounge. He graciously invited me in and we engaged in a typical conversation, inquiring about each other's children and ex-wives while he quietly warmed up for the show, playing his unplugged bass.

"I've never seen three guys make getting pussy so fucking difficult."

Bobby Dall, September 2003

Abruptly, a panic-stricken C.C. exploded through the doorway. He frantically began asking Bobby's advice regarding a situation with a woman in his dressing room next door.

"Fuck her!" Bobby commanded.

"But I can't, Bob. She's married," C.C. confessed with a sigh.

"So *now* you have a conscience?" Bobby asked. He then ordered his guitarist to "be a man" and go handle the situation. As C.C. reluctantly exited the room Bobby leaned towards me. "I've never seen three guys make getting pussy so fucking difficult," he quietly muttered with disgust.

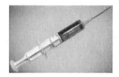

In addition to their truck catching fire, Poison's 2003 *Louder, Harder, Faster* tour endured additional dramatic close calls.

During the Orlando, Florida show at The House of Blues in August, a brawl broke out near the front of the stage and the band had to stop the show. After some persuasive coaxing on Bret's part, order finally prevailed and the show continued without a hitch.

Another incident occurred on August 23 in Omaha, Nebraska. A somewhat inebriated C.C. actually fell off the stage mid-show. Despite a bruised ego, he survived the fall.

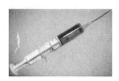

In addition to Skid Row, Poison's 2003 tour also featured opening act Vince Neil. Although the Mötley Crüe frontman was touring as a solo act with a new band, his nightly performances primarily consisted of Crüe classics. Vince was also dealing with some dark issues throughout the tour. Reportedly, Bobby had to defuse a late night situation in an Omaha hotel bar when a visibly drunk and out of control Vince began causing a scene and throwing bar glasses across the room.

Vince's behavior also reportedly proved to be problematic in Champaign, Illinois on September 7. According to radio reports there was a disagreement between Vince and Rikki backstage that night. Allegedly, Vince became enraged and physically violent. Sources further reported Vince was literally spitting and stammering as he tried to speak. While attempting to break up the scuffle, Vince reportedly grabbed Bobby by the throat, further aggravating Bobby's chronic neck injury.

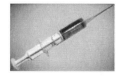

For a few years Bret had been sharing with me his plans to cross over into the thriving field of country music as a solo artist. He mentioned he had been spending considerable time performing and writing with prominent country artists like Kenny Chesney and Toby Keith. By 2004 he was in the studio recording *Freedom of Sound*, his debut as a full-fledged country artist. The official details of Bret's shift to country were to have been announced at Nashville's annual summer *Fan Fair* festival in 2004. The album finally hit stores in 2005 and met with a lukewarm response.

In addition to his solo aspirations in 2004, Bret was also preparing for Poison's upcoming summer tour with Kiss. We spoke again prior to the tour's June kickoff in San Antonio, Texas. As always, Bret was excited to get back on the road and he gladly delivered more ready-for-print one liners.

"We live by our own set of rules, the way rock and roll was meant to be."

Bret Michaels, May 2004

In February 2004 Bobby autographed this bass guitar for a celebrity golf tournament and charity auction.The event raised over $10,000 for a Florida domestic violence shelter. (Photo by Karen Madsen)

It was during my 2004 phoner with Bret that I first mentioned my intention of writing a book. Calmly, but obviously concerned about how he'd be portrayed in the possible project, Bret began offering me suggestions as to how *he* thought I should write *my* book.

Once I completed writing the 2004 feature story, I emailed a copy to Bret's assistant before it went to print. I did this only as a personal courtesy. Ever mindful of his well-crafted public image, the assistant was unhappy with my reference to Bret wearing lipstick in Poison's early days and asked me to change my story. Like I said, I advanced her the piece as a courtesy; I wasn't seeking approval. Although I've been accused of swinging from Poison's dicks many times over the years, I wasn't changing my story for anyone, not even for my buddy Bret.

Me and Bret at the after show party in Nashville on July 2, 2004.

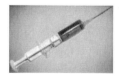

I spoke to Bobby on the phone on July 1, 2004. Poison was in the middle of their summer tour with Kiss and I was scheduled to fly from Florida to the Nashville show the following night. Anyone who's known me for any length of time knows I'm a huge Kiss fan.

Having been friends for years, Bobby was also well aware of this fact. Although I'd never been disruptive at any previous Poison function, Bobby was concerned that I might somehow embarrass him in front of Kiss. Referring to the Hebrew lineage of Kiss founders Gene Simmons and Paul Stanley, Bobby instructed me that I "was not to talk to the Jews" backstage.

I'm always mindful of where I do and do not belong in a concert setting. In fact, I made no effort to go backstage in Nashville until after Poison's set. However, despite my VIP credentials, I was stopped at the backstage gate by Big John. Although our relationship had always been friendly in the past, John actually pushed me back as I attempted to make my way backstage. One by one, guests with lesser credentials than mine were waved backstage. Before long, I was the last person left standing outside the gate. Finally, Big John brought me back to Poison's meet-and-greet, just as I heard the sound of Kiss taking the stage. Hmm, it seemed almost as if I had been intentionally detained. As I was talking to Rikki after the show, tour manager Rob Stevenson instructed me not to go back out front yet as Bobby wanted to see me. So I waited — and waited. From backstage I could hear Kiss performing their classic tunes. "Love Gun," "Deuce," "Makin' Love," and "Lick it Up" all played as I stood in the backstage hallway like a dope, missing my favorite band while I waited on Bobby Dall. Finally, after Kiss was more than half way through their show I was summoned into Bobby and C.C.'s dressing room. "I guess I've fucked up your night enough," Bobby laughingly confessed, clearly taking considerable pleasure in thwarting my Kiss experience. Fortunately Kiss was touring with a half-scab line-up in 2004 — two hired guns wearing the legendary Spaceman and Cat make-up — so I doubt I missed much. Had the *real* Ace Frenley and Peter Criss been onstage I certainly would not have allowed Bobby to dick me around.

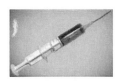

Poison took a break from touring in 2005. By the time they returned to the road in 2006 to celebrate their 20th anniversary, I had become an official member of their touring staff. As a result I was reminded of what my dad had told me when I was kid — "Be careful what you wish for in life because you just might get it!"

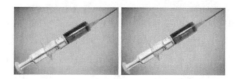

CHAPTER FOUR

CAN'T BRING ME DOWN

"It's my fucking way or the highway!" Bobby screamed at me over the phone in May 2006, clearly articulating his disapproval of an upcoming recording project in which we were both involved. Bobby had never spoken to me like this before and honestly, I was quite taken aback by his tone. But I was sure that it was an isolated meltdown and it would never happen again. I was wrong.

After years of establishing myself as a trusted ally, I was offered an official position on Poison's touring staff. I served as Bobby Dall's personal assistant on their 2006 *20 Years of Rock* summer tour. Bobby had won his battle with alcohol in the 1990s so having an assistant by his side who was also committed to sobriety was a priority for him. Having beaten my own alcohol addiction in 2004 I could relate to Bobby's need to surround himself with other non-drinkers. Although I had little touring experience at the time, Bobby and I had been friends for years. I didn't drink, I didn't smoke and I didn't do drugs. I was just competent enough to carry luggage, so the job was mine. At the age of forty-three I was finally going on my first major tour. The experience would be both amazing and unforgettable. I traveled with the band to LA, Las Vegas, Atlantic City, Chicago, St. Louis, Atlanta, Dallas, New York City and every town in between. I met lifelong musical heroes, industry insiders and incredible women. However, in the words of Charles Dickens, "It was the best of times, it was the worst of times." And I'll never look at the concert business, the music industry or even a tour bus the same way again.

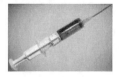

"You're just going to be Bobby's buddy for the summer," I was told by 2006 tour manager Rob Stevenson on the phone just a week or two prior to the tour's June 13 kick-off. A longtime industry veteran, Stevenson's résumé included stints with Hall and Oates, Kiss and The Rolling Stones. By 2006 Stevenson had accumulated eighteen years working with Poison, so I trusted him when he stressed that my job would involve little more than carrying luggage and going to the movies.

I first saw my name listed in pre-tour emails under the title "Tour Security." Now *that* made me laugh! If Poison was counting on me to be security we were all in BIG trouble. Don't get me wrong, I've had to throw-down before. In fact, I beat a kid's head in with a cafeteria chair in high school back in 1980. The kid was from a rival local band. He started harassing me one day in the school lunchroom — threatening that he was going to kick my ass. I warned him not to fuck with me. As I turned to walk away he punched me in the back like a little sissy. There must have been one hundred students looking on. Not wanting to be perceived by my peers as a pussy, I picked up a chair and in true WWE fashion I knocked him silly. But that had been a *very* long time ago. Now, at forty-three and standing five-foot-six, I couldn't intimidate a Hannah Montana fan, let alone one of Poison's rowdy, after-show, backstage miscreants. I assured Stevenson that as a result of my long friendship with Bobby, I knew exactly what to expect. "Yeah, right," he nervously replied. The noticeable uneasiness in Stevenson's voice should have tipped me off to the fact that he wasn't being entirely forthcoming about the job description. But even Bobby himself assured me that it would be a great experience. He also promised that if he ever did have a problem concerning me while on tour, he would handle it calmly and privately.

Fortunately, former Poison assistant Scotty Ludwick gave it to me straight. Scotty and I had become friends since first meeting in LA on Poison's 2003 tour. Recognizing my lack of major league road experience, he felt compelled to warn me about life on the road. He

graciously invited me to his Palm Bay, Florida home a few days before the tour kickoff to explain exactly what the job entailed. "These guys treat their employees like shit," Scotty quietly confessed, in his home office. He added that once the tour was over, I'd never want to do it again. And he was right... almost. While I appreciated Scotty's warnings, I wasn't about to pass up the opportunity of a lifetime.

Bobby with former Poison assistant Scotty Ludwick in 2004. (Photo by Amber Curtis)

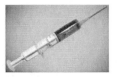

Although I had been performing and traveling for more than twenty years on an indie level with my own band, Dead Serios, touring as someone's assistant would prove to be an entirely different experience. I was accustomed to being the golden child — the star of the show. I was used to being in charge and calling the shots. In fact, Bobby and I frequently joke that in our hometown of Melbourne, I'm more famous than he is. This was a distinction that I'd pay for dearly on tour.

In the spring of 2006 there was no mention in the local press of Bobby leaving to go on tour. However, as a well-known writer, musi-

cian and popular nightclub DJ on Florida's East Coast, my involvement in the upcoming tour made front page news of our hometown paper, *Florida Today*. But on tour, Bobby was the star. And hardly a minute would pass on the road when I wasn't reminded of his status, by Bobby himself.

This ad promoting "farewell" festivities held in *my* honor at a nightclub in Palm Bay, Florida appeared in the local newspaper on June 1, 2006.

Prior to the 2006 tour, I was co-managing a twenty-year-old up-and-coming pop singer/songwriter from Cocoa Beach, Katty Pleasant. I persuaded Bobby to get involved with the project and he began co-writing songs with her. He got so involved that he also produced Katty's demo. A few days before we got on the road I scheduled a photo shoot for Katty where Bobby played a

Here I am hosting the Brevard Live Music Awards ceremony in Melbourne, Florida in August 2005. (Photo by Terry Wallace)

key creative role. After the shoot we went across the street to a seafood place for lunch. Seated at our table was the gorgeous, blond, pop princess Katty, my business partner and former Kiss business manager and author C.K. Lendt, Bobby, and myself. Toward the end of the meal, the restaurant owner approached our table. She apologized for her intrusion and then indicated that a member of her staff had notified her of a celebrity sighting at our table. "I just had to come over and see if it was true," she nervously confessed. "You're DJ Chris, aren't you?" She did not realize that to my left was a best-selling author and to my right was a multi-platinum-selling rock star.

Although I was flattered, it did create a slightly awkward moment. But Bobby laughed and shook his head. At least he appeared to be amused by my local celebrity status.

Bobby and Katty having a little fun at a 2006 photo shoot
(Photo by Kevin Roberts)

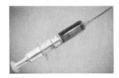

On another occasion, it was Bobby who was recognized while we had lunch at a local Mexican restaurant. Very politely, the manager notified Bobby of a diehard Poison fan sitting at a table on the opposite side of the restaurant. Upon spotting Bobby, the fan asked the restaurant manager to ask Bobby for an autograph. The manager agreed and approached Bobby with the request. Bobby agreed but told the manager he'd only honor the request if the fan paid for his lunch. Obviously joking, I started laughing at Bobby's response. Then I realized he wasn't joking. He was actually serious. I was so embarrassed I could have crawled under the table. Startled by this, the manager offered to personally pay for Bobby's meal rather than relay the crass counter-offer to Bobby's fan. In the end, the fan got the autograph, the manager appeased his customer and the million-aire rock star got a free lunch.

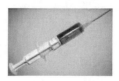

Early in 2006 Poison was preparing to record a remake of the Grand Funk Railroad classic, "We're an American Band," for the upcoming *20 Years of Rock* compilation record. The rest of his band was located on the other side of the country and Bobby needed to rehearse for the upcoming LA recording session with other live musicians. As a well-known local drummer, Bobby invited me to his place one afternoon for a jam session. It was actually rather comical. There we were, two forty-somethings, preparing for a major label recording session. We were crammed between the bed and the dress-er in the bedroom of Bobby's fifteen-year-old son Zak. I was playing Zak's kid-sized drum kit while Bobby played bass through an amp stashed in the closet. It was reminiscent of our teenage years. We could have spontaneously burst into a rousing version of "Cat Scratch Fever." In fact, we probably did. That afternoon Bobby com-mented on how talented he thought I was. Oddly, that was the last compliment I ever received from him.

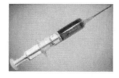

For years, I've heard musicians joke about how little talent is required to be Poison's bass player. The truth is that Bobby is an amazing, rock solid musician. I only wish that I had been able to find a player like him back in my early band days. He always has a rehearsal bass and amp set up backstage while touring and is committed to daily bass and vocal practice. It also became clear to me that Bobby is the "go-to" guy in the Poison organization. Anyone from booking agents and concert promoters to accountants and record label reps contact him with issues and concerns. In fact, I remember Enuff Z'nuff bassist, Chip Z'nuff, once waiting two hours to get fifteen minutes on the bus with Bobby. Even adult film star Ron Jeremy waited (and waited) for a chance to see Bobby after Poison's 2006 LA appearance.

"All we have in life is our reputation."

Bobby Dall, June 2006

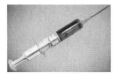

In the spring of 2006 Bobby encouraged me to contact his former mentor Kim Fowley. Recalling his early influence on Poison, Bobby thought that Fowley could offer the perfect song for Katty, the singer I was managing.

After some Internet research I located Fowley's email address. I sent him a message and it went unanswered for weeks. Then one Friday night in March, the unthinkable happened — Kim Fowley actually called my house! His name is probably unfamiliar to most, however, the sixty-six-year-old Fowley, was a rock and roll legend. At first, the idea of personally speaking with him was surreal. He's quite intimidating but I couldn't let him sense any fear. Fowley quickly and frankly admitted that he didn't like me and further suspected that I was a drug dealer, masquerading as a music manager. After explaining that I was professionally involved with Bobby Dall, Fowley paused. "Poison. I remember them," he simply responded. "Isn't Bret Michaels bald now?" he immediately inquired.

He requested I send him information on Katty and after some consideration, he'd get back to me. Although I promptly mailed the

requested materials to Fowley the next day, I never heard back from him. In fact, the only real advice that he offered regarding Katty's career was that I create a Web site featuring provocative nude photos of her. "Horny forty-year-old men could jack off to them," he suggested. Thanks for the swell advice, Kim!

Me and my business partner, C.K. Lendt with Katty, backstage following her January 2006 performance in Melbourne, Florida.

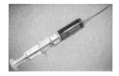

Bobby and I had several pre-tour conversations in 2006 regarding a potential book. In fact, we had a breakfast meeting at a local Cracker Barrel restaurant to specifically address this issue. From stories of encounters with LA police in the band's early days to tales of performing at the home of a European drug lord in their platinum-selling heyday, Bobby had unbelievable stories about Poison that would shock even his most loyal fans. He thought my involvement could take some of the heat off him for revealing dirt on Bret. But he was also concerned about his kids learning about the sins of his past. Ultimately, in much the same way as other projects we contemplated over the years, Bobby suddenly changed his mind about writing a book. He brought it up once during the tour and then never again, until early 2009. But by then, neither of us were interested in working together on any project.

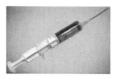

Finally, after weeks of preparation, it was time to hit the road. The night before the tour was total chaos. I spent most of that evening in my garage, organizing and preparing Bobby's guitars, golf clubs and other recreational items for loading onto the plane the next morning. The band had been rehearsing in LA for several days and while I finished packing my bags that night, I watched them perform live on *The Tonight Show*.

I called Bobby that night to congratulate him on a great performance. Weeks earlier, I expressed to my former girlfriend Karen my growing concerns for Bobby's well-being. Recently, he blamed numerous mysterious "illnesses" on a migraine condition. One afternoon he went ballistic when he noticed me standing behind him in his kitchen as he sorted through a cupboard containing various medications. Honestly, I wasn't even paying attention to what he was doing. I was looking for a bottle opener. In my darker days, my vice was alcohol so I'm a bit naïve when it comes to chemicals. However, even Helen Keller would have noticed Bobby's rambling and slurring during our final pre-tour phone conversation. Hoping for the best, I tried to reassure myself that it was just my imagination.

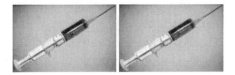

CHAPTER FIVE

NOTHIN' BUT A GOOD TIME? - The 2006 tour

There I was, doing Bret Michaels's laundry in a muggy, un-air conditioned laundromat in Clearfield, Pennsylvania on a hot August afternoon in 2006. I was sweating like a pig, trying to ignore the now continuous ringing in my ears and I began to ask myself, "Is this a glamorous gig or what?" Oh sure, Poison's *20 Years of Rock* summer tour was filled with all of the sex, drugs and rock and roll that my mom warned me about as a kid, but I got more... a lot more!

I flew into the Minneapolis airport from Melbourne, Florida and met with Bobby, C.C., Rikki, and other members of the tour entourage at 4PM on June 10. Typically, Bret rarely interacts with the rest of the band unless they're actually on stage so he arrived in Minnesota under separate travel arrangements.

Each band member had their own personal assistant or "guy" as we were called. Likewise, each assistant also referred to their respective band member as their "guy." Bret's guy was his cousin Bob Huslinger, Rikki had his business partner Brian Cocivera and Kevin Carter attended to C.C. We piled into a twelve passenger van at the airport and traveled to Mankato, Minnesota where the tour would kickoff on June 13. The crew had already been at the arena in Mankato for days, assembling the stage and fine tuning the production. The band now arrived for two days of additional preparation and rehearsal.

From the moment I stepped off the plane in Minneapolis, I noticed a change in Bobby. His demeanor immediately shifted from that of an easygoing, hometown buddy to a demanding, impatient, intolerant and distant guy whom I hardly recognized. Although I had seen this side of him right before we left home, I naïvely attributed his mood swings to pre-tour anxieties. I was convinced that he'd return to his normal self once we were settled on the road. I was wrong.

For starters, I learned that Bobby is hypoglycemic. If he doesn't eat at certain times, he gets physically ill. In fact, he typically carried energy bars in case of an emergency. During the ninety minute trip from the Minneapolis airport to the hotel in Mankato, our entourage stopped at an Applebee's restaurant. The place was busy, the service  was slow and Bobby was visibly growing impatient. Simply wanting to eat and eat quickly, Bobby had suggested we all go to a fast food joint. However, vegetarian Rikki Rockett was having no part of that. Bobby quickly became restless and began fidgeting as he sat at our large yet overcrowded booth. Finally the waitress arrived at our table but before she could take everyone's order, Bobby stormed out of the restaurant.

At the Melbourne airport in 2006 headed out on my first tour.My son was obviously less than enthusiastic about me leaving. (Photo by Karen Madsen)

"What the fuck is wrong with Bob?" Rikki asked me. At the time I had no idea what the problem was. I stood up from the table and went outside to find my guy. Ten minutes later I finally found him scarfing down Jalapeño Poppers at the Arby's restaurant next door. "Mmm! I just needed to eat," he moaned with near orgasmic satisfaction.

NOTHIN' BUT A GOOD TIME? - The 2006 Tour

During our journey to Mankato the mood in the van was, for the most part, upbeat. Rikki suggested we all make crazy hats and have "Hat Night." I was wearing a train conductor's hat and C.C. made jokes about how he was going to "pull a train" on me. It was all good fun, however, Bobby remained quiet and brooding the entire trip. I tried to lighten his mood by suggesting we hit a strip club that night. He responded by informing me that I should have "already sussed that out."

I soon learned that *lots* of things bother Bobby. Most smells bother him, most sounds bother him and most people bother him (to name just a few things).

Shortly after checking into the Mankato Holiday Inn we noticed a barking dog in one of the guest rooms across the hall from Bobby's room. Bobby was less than thrilled about this and told Rob Stevenson to resolve the issue. My rookie naïveté led me to believe that Stevenson would in fact handle the matter. I was wrong.

After checking in and dropping off luggage at the hotel, our group went next door to the Midwest Wireless Civic Center to begin two nights of pre-tour preparation with the road crew who had already been assembling the stage production.

I spent most of the first evening exploring the concert venue, familiarizing myself with the stage set up, meeting the crew and minding Bobby's son, Zak.

Very quickly, Bobby contradicted his pre-tour assurance that he'd never publicly reprimand me. Backstage he flipped out in front of a room full of crew members on the first night. Apparently he discovered that the barking dog nuisance at the hotel had not yet been resolved. "You've been standing around all night with your dick in your hand!" he screamed. I was quite surprised by his harsh reaction, considering I still hadn't been given an official job description. I was completely "green," yet I was somehow expected to automatically understand the gig and immediately respond to issues like an experi-

Tour manager Rob Stevenson with C.C. DeVille.
(Photo by Amber Curtis)

enced touring vet. Despite my "greenness" I understood "chain of command." Bobby specifically asked Rob Stevenson to handle the matter and I wasn't about to interfere with his orders. Thankfully, Stevenson did finally resolve the barking dog issue. I'm gonna miss that pooch!

Earlier in the evening I was approached by Stevenson in the arena's production office. I had barely gotten off the plane and was dressed in my usual travel garb: shorts, sneakers and a Kiss T-shirt. Stevenson handed me the personal police-style security radio I'd be using backstage for the summer. Before I could even form the words to ask how to use it, he bitch-slapped me across the face. That's right — an open-handed, five-finger slap across the face. "I expect you to wear *real* clothes while you're on *my* tour," he commanded, shaking his finger in my face like I was a naughty two-year-old. If we were in a club back home I would have popped him back. But it was a different story on the road. I wasn't going to be a troublemaker — at least not on the first night of the tour. I calmly turned and walked away. In the weeks to come Stevenson would become one of my closest allies, but holy cow, what an eye-opening introduction!

I was no longer in Podunk. This was a major national production playing the biggest arenas, festivals and amphitheaters around the country (and a few casinos and county fairs) to thousands of fans nightly. As a rookie, I recognized the need to keep pace with the "big boys" if I was going to survive. I was quickly introduced to how life on the road was really going to be for the next three months.

Kevin Carter had to snap this shot quickly before Bobby
Dall caught me with "my dick in my hand!"

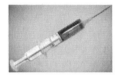

In 2006 each band member had their own bus. The four personal
assistants and four personal stage techs traveled on their respective
guy's bus. The rest of the crew traveled on a separate bus. Both the
band and the crew lived on their respective buses while performing
concerts five nights a week. We only stayed in hotels on the two
weekly off-nights.

Most modern tour buses are equipped with televisions, DVD players, stereos, sinks, cupboards, refrigerators, stoves, microwave
ovens, restrooms and showers. Typically, tour buses are designed
with a "shotgun" seat up front, next to the driver's seat. Behind those
two seats is a curtain that separates the driver's area from the rest of
the bus. Behind the curtain there is usually a front lounge area with
couches on the left and right and a narrow walkway down the middle. This walkway leads to a kitchen area and that leads to a restroom. Beyond the restroom, there is generally a sliding door which
leads to the bunk area. Most buses accommodate twelve bunks that
can best be described as coffin-like compartments with privacy cur-

tains. Typically, bunks are arranged in two sets, three high on each side of the narrow center walkway. They are just large enough to fit a six-foot-something person. However, by removing the center bunks on each side of the bus, the remaining bunks can be enlarged or "condo'd." Since only a few people traveled on Bobby's bus, our bunks were condo'd. One nice thing about tour bus bunks is that they're often equipped with miniature televisions similar to those on airplanes. Behind the bunk area is usually a rear lounge or master bedroom. The majority of the luggage and personal effects are stashed in the storage bays located beneath the bus living area.

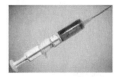

Because of our late night existence on the road, Bobby would typically sleep in until about 10 or 11AM while I'd usually roll out of the tour bus (if it was already at the venue) or hotel room to start my workday around 8AM. Before Bobby awoke I had to locate the venue's catering and dressing rooms, find the closest Starbucks, restaurants and movie theaters in each city, and acquire green bananas along with a copy of *USA Today*.

My other duties included, but were not limited to, checking into hotel rooms, lugging loads of luggage out of the bus, up flights of stairs and down endless hallways into hotel or dressing rooms, restocking tour bus supplies and organizing the guest list for that night's show. I was also expected to read Bobby's mind and know what he wanted without him asking. I'm not joking.

But my days weren't all work. Bobby and I were full-fledged caffeine junkies. Every afternoon without fail we would stop whatever we were doing and borrow a car from someone at the concert venue to make a trip to the local Starbucks coffee shop. Despite the buzz of activity surrounding the band, life backstage day in and day out can be such a mind-numbing existence that daily breaks to places like

Starbucks and local shopping malls provide a necessary intermission to keep chartbusting rock stars from going absolutely nuts.

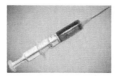

   Another touring responsibility of mine was attending to Bobby's fifteen-year-old son Zak. Zak loves to travel and he has been on the road with his father most of his life. During the summer, Zak is typically out with Bobby for entire tours. However, his younger sister Zoe preferred a more structured life at home in Florida. So while her dad is out on the road, she mainly stays at home in Melbourne with her mother, Bobby's ex- wife, Michelle. When Zoe did come out on the road it was for brief visits and she was chaperoned by either Michelle or Michelle's sister, Tanya.

Zak Dall in 2006 with adult film legend Ron Jeremy backstage in LA. (Photo by Christopher Long)

   In 2006 Bret was the only other Poison member with children. His two daughters — six-year-old Raine and one-year-old Jorja visited

75

Bret on the tour once or twice and were accompanied by their mother — Bret's longtime girlfriend, Kristi Lynn Gibson.

I'd known Zak since he was a baby and we had a real buddy-buddy relationship. In fact, we had more in common with each other than we did with people who were our respective ages. Even before I began touring with Poison, Zak and I frequently hung out, cruising the local shopping mall, going to movies and attending concerts together. Back home in Florida, I ran my own mobile DJ service and Zak often assisted me on weekends as I worked at various private parties. On the road I was as much his assistant as I was his father's. If Zak needed anything in the middle of the night, it was up to me to play "Rock Nanny" and attend to his needs.

Early one morning, Zak woke me on the bus needing to find a restroom. We had already arrived at that night's venue at Red River Valley Fairgrounds in Fargo, North Dakota. The buses were parked in the backstage area which was currently a huge, sloppy mud pit located in the middle of a race track fairway. For some reason, Zak couldn't use the facilities on the bus so I had to locate a restroom somewhere on the fairgrounds. Fortunately, I found one about one hundred yards from the bus. However, Zak's shoes were in the back lounge area of the bus where his father was sleeping and Bobby was not to be awakened. So I told Zak to jump on my back and I trudged through the mud to get him to the restroom. For this I had to endure a ribbing from the crew as they laughed, watching me carry the five-foot-seven teenager like an oversized backpack through the mud, to the restroom and back to the bus. This was another display of my commitment to my guy. Unfortunately, this type of dedication meant nothing to Bobby. It was more convenient for him to ignore what I did well. Rather, his focus was on screaming, mocking and calling me names for my "incompetence" as I struggled with other tasks.

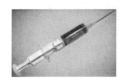

Also on my list of regular tour tasks was procuring nightly after-show babes for my guy. Above everything else, this is where I truly excel. Prior to departing on the 2006 tour, I thought I'd get a leg up on babe-related issues by lining up chicks in advance — utilizing the "friends" list on Poison's MySpace. Before we even left home, I had girls set up for Bobby in practically every major city on the tour. Unfortunately, most, if not all of the prearranged women who looked so fetching online turned out to be considerably less so in person. As a result, I needed to opt for "Plan B" on an almost nightly basis. Plan B involved distributing after-show passes to various hotties in the crowd who were Bobby's type (young, tall and slender with long, straight hair and enhanced breasts). The girls would be corralled into

a holding area by security after the show until I escorted them to Bobby's private after-show meet-and-greet. People in the touring business occasionally refer to these as "pussy passes." I, however, would never use such a derogatory term when referring to Poison's female fans. Okay, maybe I *did* say it once or twice!

Here I am in full uniform and with Sharpie in hand while on the 2006 tour, prepping that night's "pussy passes."
(Photo by Karen Colvin)

Every night, I'd comb the crowd with passes in hand. It was a constant battle to "tag" the cream of each night's female crop with "Bobby" passes before they were tagged by another band member's assistant. This was the only time I ever had an issue with any other member of the staff. A few weeks into the 2006 tour I noticed many of my finest picks weren't winding up in Bobby's after-show meet-and-greets. Nightly, I'd brag to Bobby about the stunning women I'd found for him but after the show they were nowhere to be found.

77

Somebody was obviously cock-blocking me and I became determined to get to the bottom of the situation. I soon uncovered Rikki's assistant Brian Cocivera accosting my "Bobby" girls in the crowd — removing my "Bobby" passes and replacing them with his "Rikki" passes. I told Bobby about my findings and at first I don't think he bought it, not until after the August 16 show in Charlotte, North Carolina. When the fabulous blond twins I tagged for Bobby were spotted in Rikki's meet-and-greet, I drew the line. I finally had enough of Cocivera's cock-blocking tactics. I pointed out the two beauties to Bobby and he crashed Rikki's after-show celebration. Bobby boldly entered Rikki's domain and walked the two girls right out of the party and down the hall into his dressing room. During a playful interrogation, the girls concurred that Cocivera had in fact pulled the ol' switcheroo. "Chris gave us passes," one of the girls confessed. "Then that fat guy said his passes were better," the other girl added, pointing out Cocivera. I was finally vindicated.

Although scoring chicks for rock stars on tour might sound cool to some, I thought it was a bit creepy. The creepy factor increased when I had to also start tagging teenage babes for Zak. He claimed to be too shy to initially approach girls but he sure wasn't shy once I'd done the legwork and brought them backstage. In fact, Zak was quite the ladies man. Backstage in Oklahoma I met a woman in her thirties whom I wanted to pursue. Zak, however seemed to be trying to hit on the same woman. I would never have expected at forty-three to be competing for an adult woman with a fifteen-year-old boy. Hilarious! FYI — I won.

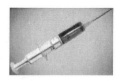

One thing Bobby hates (almost) more than anything is misinformation. Thus, I was under constant pressure to get everything right, which is an impossible task for anyone. Unfortunately for me, I had fucked up just enough and early enough in the tour that after only the first few days I could no longer complete a sentence before Bobby would blurt out "Wrong! You're wrong!" But how can you be an effective employee when you know every move you make is going to be the wrong move? Of course I became a proverbial deer in the headlights whenever he'd ask me a question — I was doomed no matter how I responded.

But Bobby's an important man with an important job so when I did screw up (which apparently was often), I tried not to take his reprimands personally. In fact, in my professional life, I've often been accused of treating people in the same nasty, impatient and condescending way as he was treating me. I understood the pressures of being an artist. Hopefully, once we returned home, all would be forgotten and we would return to being buddies. In the meantime, our relationship on the road would remain strained.

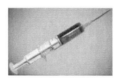

Early in the tour I discovered an assortment of prescription drugs in one of Bobby's carry-on bags. From stomach meds and painkillers to Ambien and Xanax, the contents of Bobby's bag resembled a traveling pharmacy. To me, it explained his erratic behavior. A longtime close friend of Bobby's, production manager Mark Hogue, pulled me aside following the show in Rapid City, South Dakota and questioned me about Bobby's well-being. I tried to dissuade his concerns by maintaining that Bobby seemed fine. I seriously doubt Hogue bought my story.

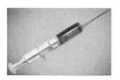

Although Bobby's eyesight isn't any better than mine, he took to calling me "Mr. Magoo," a half-blind, bumbling cartoon character from the 1960s. One crew member joked that, "Bobby's 'seeing eye dog' needed a seeing eye dog." Bobby further insisted that my hearing was also a problem — okay, I'll give him that one. But c'mon, he even mocked me for how I ate. He also was amused by how I walked, prompting him to refer to me as "Twinkle Toes."

"I can be such an asshole."

Bobby Dall, June 2006

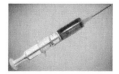

Despite my apparent incompetence, I always tried my best to take care of my guy. But I quickly realized that the more I produced, the more Bobby demanded. Playing the "disability card" helped to lower his expectations and keep him off my back a bit.

Bobby was entertaining a few guests in his dressing room prior to Poison's show at New York's Jones Beach Amphitheater in August. From an adjacent room I could hear him mocking me — laughing as he bet his friends that I wouldn't hear him if he called my name. So I played along, ignoring him as he summoned me. They all got a big kick out of Bobby's bumbling, impaired assistant. But I didn't care, the tour was nearly over and I'd soon be headed home.

However, Rikki came to my defense during the tour. He made clear to Bobby that he personally had no problem with my abilities.

C.C. and Bobby onstage in Hartford, Connecticut on August 9, 2006
(Photo by Sandy Creamer)

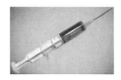

CHAPTER FIVE

Touring *can* be a fabulous experience if you're in the touring band. Also, if you are a tag-along like a girlfriend, boyfriend or buddy of a band member, traveling on tour for a day or two with no responsibilities, it can be an absolute blast. However, it's a completely different story if you're a working member of the tour's staff.

As a crew member or personal assistant working on a major tour you are there to benefit the band. Period. Crew members maintaining their own agenda are either reprimanded or replaced. So unless you're actually in the band, life on the road ain't always the party that it's perceived to be. The hours are long and the work is demanding. In fact, with the exception of the few hours a night spent sleeping in your bunk on the bus and the two weekly days off, the work on tour is practically non-stop.

As a personal assistant, I worked harder on the off days than on show days. Even if there was no concert scheduled on a particular night, my guy still needed to be checked into his hotel. His bags, snacks, computer gear and other personal effects all needed to be moved from the bus to his room. Plus, he has to be entertained while enjoying a relaxing day off in Anytown, USA. It was my responsibility to know the location of certain restaurants, shopping malls, movie theaters, and tourist attractions in every city if I was going to keep my guy fed and happy.

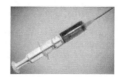

I realized in 2006 many of the rock classics I listened to as a kid were in fact, crash courses in life on the road. Listen to "Turn the Page." Seger was right — being on tour can really be a lonely experience. And yes, people actually do make snide comments when you walk into a truck-stop or restaurant, especially at 3AM. But there's also an unglamorous side to life on the road that's *not* romanticized in old Bob Seger songs. That's the area concerning personal needs and privacy. Unless you are in the band, you have no privacy on the road.

While in Dallas on July 7, I was lucky enough to grab an early shower. As I was rinsing the shampoo out of my hair I got the eerie feeling of being watched. I opened my eyes to discover Bobby goofing around, peering over the top of the shower curtain trying to cop a peek at my "stuff." Although he jokingly complimented me on the size of my penis, I was still disappointed that I wasn't afforded the opportunity to "chub up" first! Oddly, the incident wasn't an isolated one. In fact, there is hardly a time working on Poison tours when crew members aren't being watched by somebody.

On tour, one's sense of modesty is something to be left at home. For instance, Bobby has no shame regarding personal needs. He would frequently walk around on his bus or in his dressing room completely naked — shaving his balls or with a towel hanging from his erect penis as if they were completely natural things to do. At first I was a bit taken aback by Bobby's boldness, but looking back, it was pretty funny!

Bret Michaels onstage front and center with Poison on August 9, 2006 in Hartford, Connecticut.
(Photo by Sandy Creamer)

Except for days off, everybody on the crew lives, works, eats and sleeps together. Utilities we take for granted at home are precious luxuries on the road. For example, some of the outdoor festivals Poison played didn't provide running water backstage. In fact, sometimes there wasn't even a backstage. Occasionally, the tour buses were simply parked in the grass behind an unsecured stage area. The combination of no running water with a non-stop work load can prohibit crew members from showering or even going to the bathroom at their liberty.

Although tour buses are equipped with showers, they don't carry enough water for a dozen showers. One Poison tour staff member once confided to me that due to the non-stop demands of her particular job she often had to go several days without showering.

Then there is the infamous Tour Rule #1, "No shitting on the bus." As a result, tour bus toilets are (for some purposes) also off limits. Unfortunately, there is the occasional tour bus whose residents don't adhere to Rule #1 and the sweltering summer heat intensifies the sulfurous stench permeating from the waste receptacle.

Being constantly on the go and sweating all day in the summer heat, it's not unusual for some crew members to develop a painful variation of diaper rash, un-affectionately known as "gigbutt." Also, early in the 2006 tour, the blisters on my feet were so bad I could barely walk. Consequently, after the first week of the tour Bobby saw to it that I traded in my boots for a pair of sneakers.

The undesirable conditions don't end there. Not all hotels have laundry facilities. Although Janna was Poison's full-time wardrobe manager in 2006, she was not hired to do the crew's laundry. The opportunity for the crew to occasionally wash clothes on tour becomes a personal joy. Upon checking into hotels, crew members would often race each other for first dibs on available washing machines.

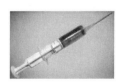

On the other hand, touring doesn't always suck. From masseuses, hair stylists and tattoo artists, to chefs and doctors, there is never a shortage of people available backstage to pamper the members of Poison. As a personal assistant I often experienced many of the same perks as the band members. I stayed in the nicest suites, enjoyed the best food and hung out with some groovy VIPs. Also, somehow strangers knew my name. "That's Chris, he's Bobby's assistant," I frequently overheard people say as I'd walk through concert halls and hotel lobbies. It was weird and a little bit unsettling.

Rikki Rockett onstage in Hartford, Connecticut on August 9, 2006 (Photo by Sandy Creamer)

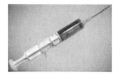

One perk I discovered in 2006 was when you're on tour with a major act, you can ask for anything and somebody will bring it to you. Bobby didn't like the toaster on his bus so I told production assistant Karen Colvin. An hour later Bobby had his new toaster.

CHAPTER FIVE

C.C. enjoys a regimented daily workout program while on tour. One morning while we were staying at The Harris Ranch Inn in Lemoore, California, C.C. came to me, pleading for a new treadmill. He indicated how impressed he was with my ability to get things done and asked me to handle the situation. Immediately, I had a dialogue with Rob Stevenson and when we got to the next city C.C. had his new treadmill.

In Phoenix, Bobby commented to the house chef at The Cricket Pavilion how much he enjoyed the bread served with that night's dinner. He also told the chef how disappointed he was that there was no more bread when he went back for seconds. By the time Bobby finished the show that night, three fresh loaves had been placed on his bus.

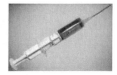

As in the movie *Almost Famous*, almost everybody has a unique nickname on tour. On Poison's crew alone we had fabulous and colorful characters like Hammer, Papa Smurf, Miami, Spidey, and Fi-Fi. Bobby's bass tech, John Popplewell, took to calling me "Chalupa," a reference to my favorite Taco Bell food item. And yes, girls do follow the band from town to town and from state to state. In fact, I can tell what part of the country I'm in depending on which chicks are hanging around the band's backstage area.

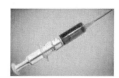

Rain or shine the show went on every night. Trust me, we saw both rain and shine under extreme circumstances. While playing an outdoor show on June 24 in Fargo, North Dakota it rained so hard that the entire band and crew were soaked to the bone by the end of the show. The rain was so intense that our buses got stuck backstage and had to be towed out of the mud by tractors after the show. In Memphis on August 26, the heat was so extreme that paramedics had to provide the band with oxygen masks backstage to get them through the show. Summertime in the Midwest also boasts flying grasshopper-like bugs. They're often so thick that outdoor gigs become almost unbearable.

It took hours for tractors to pull our tour buses out of the mud following the show in Fargo, North Dakota. (Photo by Kevin Carter)

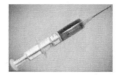

Fans attending multiple dates on concert tours may notice that it seems like the same songs are played each night on the house sound system in between band performances, and that's absolutely correct. Everything on a major tour is orchestrated, timed and calculated from the moment the doors open until the headliner finishes their encore.

From the moment the last of the opening acts completed their nightly set, each of Poison's personal assistants informed their guy of the minutes remaining until show time based on Rob Stevenson's instruction, delivered via the security radios. I enjoyed listening to backstage, pre-show jokes over the radios between the various band members like classic Henny Youngman one-liners (e.g., "Take my wife... please!"). Bobby and I also had fun with the radios as he gave us radio nicknames. He was known as Tightie Whitey and I was Secret Squirrel.

The anthemic chords of "Highway to Hell" blasting from the mega-watt, front-of-house PA system were the nightly battle call rallying it was time for Poison to rock. Since we couldn't always hear the intro to this AC/DC classic backstage, Stevenson would instruct the assistants to immediately call their guy to the stage by announcing "highway, highway" over the security radios. This magical catch phrase echoed throughout the backstage area as each assistant repeatedly hollered "highway, highway!" while gathering the band members and leading them to the stage.

C.C. DeVille onstage in Hartford, Connecticut on August 9, 2006 (Photo by Sandy Creamer)

Throughout the tour, I was rarely more than a few feet from Bobby at any given moment and show time was no exception. Each night, I'd lead him from the dressing room to the stage with my required pocketful of condiments (e.g., Orbit spearmint gum, Halls lozenges, Carmex lip balm, ear plugs, Band-Aids, Rolaids, sunglasses and guitar picks), a towel over my shoulder, a water bottle in one hand and my official "security dude" flashlight in the other. I remained side-stage throughout the show, ready to see to his every need.

For me, show time was the most exciting time of the day. And with nightly attendance often exceeding 10,000 enthusiastic fans, the roar of the crowd as the house lights dropped was often deafening. Boasting an array of chart-topping hits from their twenty-plus year career combined with enough pyro to launch a third world army and enough lighting and amperage to power a small city, Poison's 2006 live show was as exciting, bombastic and energetic as any production they'd staged before. Much of the band's spectacular nightly pyrotechnics were detonated a few feet from where I was positioned onstage. If Bobby thought I was deaf and blind at the beginning of the tour, I was really impaired by the end. With the final chord of the classic show-ending hit "Talk Dirty to Me" still ringing, I'd have Bobby headed back to his dressing room to cool off with a relaxing post-concert shower. Once I verified that his late night dinner was waiting for him on the bus, I'd begin the process of gathering his after-show guests and placing them in a predetermined holding area backstage (usually an unused catering room). As soon as I finished walking Bobby through the nightly post-concert meet-and-greet, we'd return to the bus for a quick bite. Then I'd bring Bobby's luggage from the dressing room and reload it back on the bus. Our driver Em Lehman would arrive on the scene at approximately 2AM. With keyboardist Charlie Lawrence, John Popplewell and Zak, we'd depart for another city to do it all over again the following day.

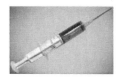

Despite my rookie status, I was treated like a pro and with total respect by the veteran crew members. Lighting director Mark "Fi-Fi" Miller welcomed me with a copy of *The Rock Snob's Dictionary* — perfect reading for a hopeless music nerd like myself. Realizing I was a huge Kiss fan, John Popplewell gave me a beautiful collection of poster-size black and white photos that he had taken of Kiss in concert. I also enjoyed getting to know Charlie Lawrence, Poison's 2006 keyboard player. He and I shared a passion for classic R&B and we often chatted about our favorite old-school performers. I felt bad because as the "new guy" learning the ropes, I always seemed to unintentionally do Charlie wrong. I'd frequently cut him off as he tried to get onstage or I'd forget to order a particular snack item for him to have on the bus. However, Charlie was always cool to me.

I was in Bobby's dressing room prior to show time on July 6 at the Zoo Amphitheater in Oklahoma City. I noticed how the backstage area more closely resembled a kid's summer camp than a rock show venue. Not wanting to forget the experience, I started writing down various details regarding the facility in my pocket notebook.

"Hey!" a stage tech shouted as he nearly knocked the notebook from my hands. "Don't forget about the confidentiality clause you signed when you joined this tour."

"I didn't sign shit," I passionately informed the usually mild-mannered musician. "The only reason I took this gig was so I could write a book," I added.

Although I did hear a slight grumble or two more about the subject from the tech during the remaining weeks of the tour, not much else was said about my note taking.

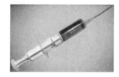

To keep going every day, Bobby and I relied on generous doses of the energy drink, Red Bull. At night, between the sporadic motion of the tour bus and still being "pumped" on "The Bull," it was often difficult to fall asleep. Consequently, Bobby introduced me to a prescription sleep aid called Ambien. Although Ambien is widely prescribed and its fabled side effects like sleepwalking have become the center of considerable controversy, it was new to me in 2006. I've always had reservations about experimenting with any drug, but Bobby assured me that Ambien was non-addictive. Yeah, of course not!

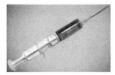

For me, life on the road is often so stressful that I rarely eat on tour. After two weeks into my first tour in 2006 I casually mentioned to one of the more experienced crew guys that I was losing a lot of weight and I felt as if I was perpetually walking on a trampoline. He kindly pointed out that I was a dumb-ass who was existing almost entirely on caffeine and sleeping pills.

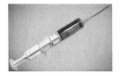

Another strength of mine was keeping Bobby's bus stocked with tasty frozen treats. Our onboard freezer always overflowed with ice cream bars, ice cream sandwiches, fudgesicles, popsicles, dreamsicles, strawberry crunch bars, Klondike Bars, and other frozen delights. Once everyone else had crashed for the night Bobby and I would enjoy what I called our nightly "Ambien Sundaes." We'd each pop a sleep aid, select our frozen treat(s) and finally relax. It was always tranquil on the bus at that time of night. Ah, peace and quiet. Bobby would usually crash right after consuming his treats while I would frequently ride shotgun with Em until I felt myself melting into the windshield. But even something as seemingly mild as an Ambien and ice cream combo can lead to problems. One night as we were leaving Las Vegas, Bobby took his sleep med a bit too early. As we passed the outskirts of town Em pulled the bus over so we could enjoy the incredible view. In one direction you could see the fabulous lights of the big city. In the other direction there was nothing but pitch black darkness and barren desert. Suddenly somebody asked, "Where's Bobby?" I looked up and in the distance I spotted the staggering silhouette of a loopy Bobby Dall wandering into the desert. "C'mon boss," I said as I walked him back to the bus. "Let's get you to bed."

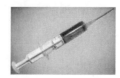

In 2006 Bobby was renting his four bedroom house, located in a gated community in Melbourne, to one of his neighbors who was having his own house renovated. Consequently, when the tour played Florida and Bobby and I got a day off in our hometown, he had to stay at a hotel. I checked Bobby into his room at the Crowne Plaza Hotel in Indialantic at 2AM on Monday, August 21. We both had homes within a couple of miles of the hotel. Taking full advantage of a night in my own bed, I had a woman already waiting for me at my place when we arrived in town. Although Bobby had already taken his late night meds, he wouldn't fall asleep and wouldn't let me leave his room. When working for Bobby, you're never off duty while he's awake and this night he just wouldn't pass out. At one point I noticed Bobby sitting on the edge of his bed with his head bobbing in an Ambien haze, hypnotized by a "feed the hungry" infomercial. Finally, my golden opportunity to escape! I ever so quietly tiptoed out the door and sprinted down the hall and out of the hotel. A buddy of mine had dropped my car off for me at the hotel earlier in the day so in no time I was back home, in my own bed, with my special new friend.

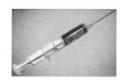

I, too, experienced an Ambien mishap, albeit an innocent one. Shortly after medicating one night in 2006 while en route from San Francisco to LA, I noticed a full apple pie in the bus fridge. I remember being the only one on the bus still awake and being a bit loopy as I leaned over the sink of the kitchenette, devouring a delicious slice of pie — then I blacked out. When I awoke the next morning I discovered an empty pie tin in the sink and I was covered in apple pie residue. Mmm, pie!

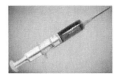

In 2006, I spent a lot of time late at night talking to our bus driver Em. He had been on tours since the 1960s and he was a treasure trove of road stories. From Bruce Springsteen to Johnny Cash, Em had worked with nearly everyone in the music world and as a rookie, I absorbed his many tales like a sponge. Realizing that I was a political junkie and American history buff, Em would point out various points of interest throughout our summer long journey. As we were leaving Dallas, Texas at 2AM on July 8, Em drove the bus downtown and let me stand in the very spot where JFK had been shot in Dealey Plaza. It was an eerie experience. Thanks, Em!

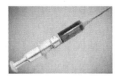

In 2006 I also discovered the role that the Internet plays on tour. From the kids in the opening act Endeverafter to Poison's production team, staying connected online at all times was crucial. With the popularity of digital and cell phone cameras, any backstage activity could wind up on the World Wide Web almost instantly. Via the Internet, any fan getting a photo with any pop/rock star at any band's meet-and-greet can easily create the illusion of a more intimate encounter than what actually took place. In fact, Bobby instructed his girlfriend Meghan to stay off music-related Web sites like MetalSludge.tv in 2006. He warned that it was all "bullshit" and what she'd find online would only upset her.

CHAPTER FIVE

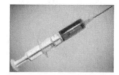

My first official touring experience was, to say the least, unforgettable. I saw more titties and ate more breakfast bars on my first tour than I did in my entire previous forty-three years. When it was over it took weeks to decompress and adjust to the "real" world. I didn't know what had just happened, but I knew that I'd been everywhere and seen everything. Throughout the entire journey I maintained focus on my guy. While others on the tour were partying, getting laid, getting high and having a good ol' time, I remained professional and centered. I didn't even partake of a single freaking blow job all summer. I did, however, collect a lot of phone numbers on the road and I quickly made up for lost time upon my return home, flying chicks from across the country at a feverish pace in and out of my place in Florida. In fact, between my new tour "friends" and the local girls

who apparently were turned on by my new big league experiences, I seriously contemplated putting a revolving door on the front of my house to keep the "traffic" flowing smoothly. But Scotty Ludwick was right. Touring was something that I'd never do again. Well...

For my hard work and dedication I was awarded this Poison gold record in 2006

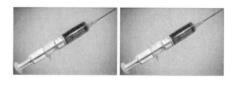

CHAPTER SIX

#1 BAD BOY(S) - The Showdown in Atlanta

I first became aware of friction between Bobby and Bret back in 2001. I was speaking to Bobby on the phone during Poison's *Glam Slam Metal Jam* tour and asked him how things were going. "Everything is great," he half-heartedly responded. "I just hope that I can get through it without murdering my lead singer."

In 2006, relations between the two rival band members became so strained that Bobby predicted weeks before we left home that we wouldn't even complete all sixty-two dates on the upcoming summer outing. But the tour went off as scheduled and Bobby and Bret did manage to complete all of the dates, but not before treating their fans to a little incident that I've come to refer as the "Showdown in Atlanta."

According to Bobby, when Poison first started in the 1980s he and Bret were great friends and truly enjoyed their early success. Going into the 2006 tour, however, they couldn't seem to agree on anything, from business strategy to songwriting. Bobby recalled Bret started "going crazy" around the time they were recording their third record, *Flesh and Blood*. Bret fights a lifelong daily battle as an insulin-dependent diabetic. Bobby once speculated that he thought that diabetes was "eating away Bret's brain." In fact, as the tour's June 13 kick-off date drew closer, Bobby was so overwhelmed with anxieties regarding interacting with Bret all summer that he was literally becoming physically ill. Although each band member travels in his own personal tour bus, the level of disdain the two had for each other had become so intense Bobby instructed his personal bus driver to never even park Bobby's bus next to Bret's.

As the tour marched on, the scorching temperature wasn't the only thing heating up. Everyone within the tour staff realized Bobby and Bret were reaching their respective boiling points. In fact, during the last two weeks of the tour Bobby and Bret were openly taunting each other. Bobby would get his digs in directly by doing silly things like making me join him in parading around Bret's bus wearing funny hats and crazy outfits. Bret's attacks, on the other hand, were not as direct. He chose to get out his frustrations by making various ridiculous demands of his band and staff members. One such rule was that all onstage crew members must be smiling at all times during the show.

With only six dates remaining on the tour the band performed a private corporate show on August 24 for the buyers of the national chain of Walmart retail stores at the Opryland theme park hotel in Nashville, Tennessee. At this point Bobby and Bret were clearly looking for any excuse to throw-down. Having had previous experience with corporate gigs as a solo artist, Bret felt that he needed to "trim some fat" from that night's set list by cutting out the individual solos by C.C. and Rikki. He also planned to eliminate "I Hate Every Bone in Your Body But Mine," a song by C.C. Bobby was, to say the

(From L to R) Kevin Carter, C.C. DeVille, Bobby Dall and myself on August 24, 2006 enjoying the riverboat ride that runs through the Opryland Hotel lobby one day before the "showdown.".

least, unhappy about the alterations and openly discussed the issue with Bret via the band's backstage security radio system. From his dressing room Bobby suggested to Bret, who was on the bus, that in the interest of "trimming fat" the band should also eliminate Bret's in-between-song banter.

"What do you mean, Bob?" Bret asked. "Are you talking about when I talk to the people in between the songs?"

"Yes. That's exactly what I'm fucking talking about!" Bobby fired back.

Bret proceeded to sarcastically announce to all staff members that since Bobby was now calling the shots regarding that night's set list, the band was going to play every song that they had ever recorded. He also warned the band to be prepared because they were going to, "play 'em all and play 'em fast!"

"As soon as I ever start to just go through the motions I'll quit."

Bret Michaels, March 2002

Upon hearing this, Bobby went crazy. He sent food trays flying and shattered a full- length mirror. "Fuck that piece of shit!" he screamed as he trashed his dressing room.

Realizing the tour was now finished for certain, I exited Bobby's dressing room and bid farewell to Janna Elias who had been stand-ing close by. "It's been great working with you," I said as I shook her hand. But, to my amazement, the band not only went on to perform that night, but they were filled with such fire and rage that it was one of the best shows of the tour!

Although there had been a feeling of impending doom throughout the entire tour, that feeling was overwhelming the following day in Atlanta, Georgia on August 25.

While in Nashville the previous day, Bobby, C.C., Kevin Carter and I visited the Bass Pro Shop located next to The Opryland Hotel. Raising suspicions, Bobby bought all sorts of ridiculous gear. Now if you're Ted Nugent, it makes perfect sense to pop in a sporting goods store and purchase a few items for the upcoming hunting season while on tour. But if you're Bobby Dall, it's a bit odd to purchase hunting hats, full-body camouflage suits and a giant-sized stuffed catfish.

In a silly attempt to get back at Bret from the previous night in Nashville, Bobby instructed me to parade around Bret's bus carrying a giant stuffed catfish while he marched around backstage wearing a full-body camouflage suit on the afternoon of the infamous "Showdown in Atlanta." (Photos by Karen Colvin)

In hopes of annoying Bret, Bobby instructed me to parade around Bret's bus all afternoon in Atlanta carrying the huge catfish. Rikki was not amused. "What the fuck is up with the fish?" he inquired as he confronted me in the catering room during lunch. I quickly informed him my actions were per Bobby's instruction. The guys from opening act Cinderella, on the other hand, were quite amused by the "pre-showdown" shenanigans. In fact, when Bobby arrived in the catering room looking like a human tree in his new full-body camouflage suit, Cinderella guitarist Jeff LaBar suggested that Bobby should have bought a miniature camouflage suit for me. That way, there would be "a little tree following around a big tree all day."

Tension filled the air behind the scenes as Poison took the stage in Atlanta that night in front of 18,000 fans at the Hi-Fi Buys Amphitheater. During the show, another member of the staff told me Bret had made derogatory comments about the other band members over the mic during the night's seventy-five minute show. But it was when Bret came side-stage during Rikki's drum solo (something he'd not done during the entire tour) and began mingling with Bobby's personal female guests that Bobby became enraged.

By the last few days of the tour it became my job to go onstage each night and introduce the band for their encore. This night would be different. With a deranged look in his eye, Bobby pushed me aside and walked onstage to introduce the band himself. In horror, I stood side-stage with Janna and stage manager Junior Jones and watched the drama unfold. Like a madman, Bobby began screaming over the mic, "Do you wanna hear some more fucking Poison?" I leaned over to Janna and whispered in her ear, "Oh shit. This isn't good." The audience, however, was totally unaware of the behind-the-scenes drama and cheered for Bobby in full force.

As the band kicked into their encore, "Talk Dirty to Me," Bret realized his mic wasn't on. Instead of allowing front-of-house sound engineer Tim Lawrence two seconds to make the necessary adjustment, Bret threw his mic across the stage, striking Bobby. At that point it was officially "go time." Bobby whipped off his bass and began swinging it violently by the strap like he was winding up for a game winning pitch. He let it fly across stage, consequently striking

Bret in the leg. The two Hair Metal poster boys then charged each other and exchanged blows. Initially I couldn't believe what I was seeing.

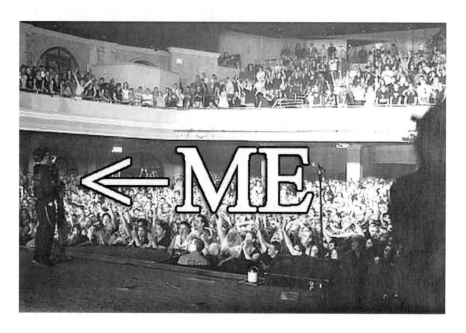

Here I am onstage introducing Poison in Orlando on August 22, 2006 (Photo by Kevin Carter)

I knew something like this was bound to happen sooner or later but when it finally did, I was dumbfounded. As soon as I saw Kevin Carter running onstage I knew it was no joke. I then ran out to help break up the fight. I rushed to Bobby's side, put my arm around him and whispered in his ear, "We're not gonna do this," as I walked him off the stage. As a bystander, the incident seemed to unfold in slow motion, lasting several minutes. After watching the video the next day on YouTube, however, I realized it happened in mere seconds.

"I want some fucking security back here, Mark!" Bobby shouted at production manager Mark Hogue as he and Rob Stevenson rushed to Bobby's side backstage.

Always putting business first, the band surprisingly went back onstage to finish the encore. Once Bret had made his way back to the mic, he apologized for *Bobby's* behavior. "You have just witnessed Poison's last show," he announced to the crowd. But little did Bret know that other members of Poison had no intention of missing the following night's concert in Memphis, Tennessee. In fact, for weeks prior to the "showdown," I was the keeper of an ever-growing list of possible replacement singers that Bobby and C.C. had been creating in the event of a mid-tour blowout with Bret. From arena rockers like Warrant frontman Jani Lane and Slaughter's Mark Slaughter to more contemporary vocalists like Butch Walker, Fuel's Brett Scallions and Dishwalla's J.R. Richards, Bobby and C.C.'s "wish list" featured dozens of candidates.

Although you could practically hear a pin drop in the backstage hallways of Atlanta at the show's conclusion, things were all abuzz in Bobby's dressing room. Production staff and band members darted in and out, discussing the incident and making calls to various replacement prospects. Skid Row frontman Johnny Solinger was available and accepted the offer to join Poison temporarily for the following night's show in Memphis.

Frequently, Janna videotaped each night's show on the 2006 tour. Moments after the Atlanta scuffle, Bobby cornered her in the hallway outside his dressing room and literally forced her to surrender the video tape of that night's show. "Give me the fucking tape!" he commanded. With the video recorder still in hand, she opened the device, removed the tape and reluctantly gave it to Bobby. A few days later, Bobby mailed the videotape to VH-1 where it soon aired as part of a "breaking news" report. About half an hour after the show we were informed Bobby allegedly injured Bret's leg during the onstage brawl and Bret was being rushed by ambulance to the hospital. Concerned about potential criminal charges for assault, it was decided that Bobby would be put aboard his own bus and rushed across the Georgia state line into Tennessee. Kevin Carter was an off-duty North Carolina police officer and would accompany Bobby to the next show in Memphis and run interference with the Atlanta police if they arrived on the scene. I stayed behind at the venue to attend to C.C. I would travel with him to Memphis later that night on his bus while finalizing arrangements on the phone with Solinger.

Typically, there were few offstage sightings of Cinderella's frontman Tom Keifer during the 2006 tour. However, the incident between Bret and Bobby was such a big deal that even he came off his bus after the show in Atlanta to investigate.

"I'm just glad that I'm not the one in trouble this time!" C.C. declared in front of a group of crew members and tag-alongs who had assembled outside of his bus in the backstage area prior to our departure. While en route from Atlanta to Memphis, our bus stopped for fuel. As C.C. and I rummaged around inside the truck stop convenience store, Rikki's bus pulled into the same service station. Rikki entered the store and spoke with C.C. in the candy aisle, about the evening's events. Rob Stevenson then entered the store and instructed them to stay there, informing them Bret would soon arrive at the truck stop and wanted to talk to them both.

Rikki Rockett live onstage with Poison in 2006 (Photo by Sandy Creamer)

Within seconds, Bret's bus pulled into the service station and C.C. panicked. "Where's my bus, Chris Long?" he nervously asked me. "I don't want to talk to him. Get me on my bus and let's get out of here." Rikki, however, remained behind and discussed business with Bret well into the wee hours.

Many unanswered questions lingered the next morning as the crew began setting up the stage at Mud Island Amphitheater in Memphis, Tennessee. Was Poison still a band? If so, who was the singer? Would the promoter that night even accept a Poison date without Bret Michaels? In fact, with only Bobby and C.C.'s buses on the Mud Island property, and considering his late night meeting with Bret, we weren't even sure whether Rikki was going to show up at the gig. However, by 1PM both Rikki and Bret's buses had arrived on the scene.

Within minutes, a private meeting between the four band members convened on Bret's bus. A funny thing about Poison is that no matter how much they want to kill each other, it's always business first. Two hours later, the members emerged from Bret's bus and announced that all four band members would perform together that night. They also ensured they would complete the tour as scheduled. Although there were only four dates remaining, there was no way that they were going to forfeit any revenue. I discovered Janna that afternoon sitting on the ground outside of the venue, literally in tears from the events of the night before. Although she technically worked for the band, she was Bret's closest ally and confidante, even working as his off-tour personal assistant. Bret was reportedly furious at her for giving the videotape to Bobby, though she feared Bobby's wrath if she didn't comply with his orders. After working for Poison for several years, she had considerable love and respect for all four band members. Unfortunately, she was now caught in the crossfire of one of their most bitter intra-band battles.

In the meantime I had another problem on my hands. I received a call on my cell phone telling me that Johnny Solinger had arrived at the Memphis venue from Texas and was waiting for me in a car parked near the buses in the backstage parking lot. I then went to

Mark Hogue's office and was given an envelope containing $5,000 cash. Although the grievances within Poison had been temporarily reconciled, a deal was a deal and Solinger was still entitled to his agreed pay whether he performed or not. I was then instructed to take the money to Solinger and suggest he check into his hotel to await information regarding his flight back to the Lone Star State the next day.

As I approached his rental car in the backstage parking lot I couldn't help but laugh. Sitting in the front passenger seat with his long blond hair and wearing a bandana and shades, Solinger looked like Bret's long lost twin brother. He was also parked in plain view, directly in front of Bret's bus.

Skid Row frontman Johnny Solinger (L) was a dead ringer for Bret (R) and would have likely been an excellent replacement. (Solinger photo by Christine Herb - Bret photo by Kevin Carter)

I introduced myself to Solinger, paid him his money, apologized for the inconvenience and made arrangements for him to meet with Bobby and me for coffee at the local Starbucks. Understandably, he was disappointed that he didn't get the gig with Poison but I guess, "it was a great paid vacation."

Meanwhile, as the show approached, the atmosphere behind-the-scenes in Memphis grew tense. Exploiting his alleged injuries for all they were worth, Bret joined the band onstage that night on crutches and wearing a leg brace. Despite Bret's limping from one side of the stage to the other during the show, not much was made of the Atlanta incident while onstage in Memphis. Things quickly returned to a business as usual status for the band and crew. In fact, I was surprised when I noticed Bret and Bobby standing side by side backstage, calmly talking to each other during C.C.'s guitar solo. After all the tension, after all the drama, after all the name calling all summer long, the two embraced and actually kissed each other! I couldn't believe my eyes. They looked more like prom dates than arch rivals!

CHAPTER SIX

CHAPTER SEVEN

PLAY DIRTY - *Mystery, intrigue and nasty odors*

My all-time favorite movie is director Cameron Crowe's Oscar-nominated 2000 film, *Almost Famous*. The movie tells the compelling behind-the-scenes story of a teenage journalist on tour in 1973 with Stillwater — a fictitious, hard working rock and roll band on the brink of stardom. As a rock writer myself, albeit a much older one, I could identify on many levels with the lead character, William Miller. I was also fascinated by the jealous, egomaniacal, paranoid and petty characteristics of the onscreen band members. After working on a few real life tours I've discovered that the film was closer to a documentary than a work of fiction.

Man of Mystery

I quickly discovered on the 2006 tour that I would see very little of forty-three-year-old frontman Bret Michaels while on the road. He typically never came to sound check with the band and rarely stayed in a hotel with the band — opting instead to remain on his bus. In fact, except for catching an occasional glimpse of the reclusive lead singer throwing the football around or working out backstage, I rarely saw Bret offstage. He spent most of his time holed-up, moni-toring the daily backstage goings on by peering out the window of his tour bus lounge. Bret was also known to frequently summon band and crew members to his bus for private lambastings if he took issue with any of his surreptitious observations of them. Bobby once warned me in 2006 that despite my amicable relationship with Bret, I too should expect to be summoned at some point while on tour. And I was.

Bret Michaels making a rare sound check appearance in Oklahoma City on July 6, 2006. (Photo by Kevin Carter)

The second show on Poison's 2006 tour took place on June 14 in Burlington, Iowa. An estimated 20,000-plus fans attended the county fair-type outdoor event. Bobby indicated that he was interested in receiving a pre-show blow job that evening so I took a walk through the crowd in search of attractive women to bring backstage. I was approached by two enthusiastic female twenty-somethings who were clearly interested in "partying" with the band. I brought them to Bobby's tour bus which was parked in the secured backstage area. As I was instructing them to wait outside the bus pending Bobby's approval, I heard a voice from over my shoulder. "Psst. Hey Chris. Hey, up here, it's me, Bret!" I looked behind me to discover Bret, way up-high, sticking his head out from the window of the bus parked next to Bobby's. "Hey, c'mon on up. I need to talk to you," he urged. I didn't know how long he had been watching me, but it was clear that on just the second night of the tour I was already being officially "summoned."

"How's it going?" Bret quickly asked as he brought me on board his bus. I told him that everything was great and after exchanging a few additional pleasantries, he cut to the chase. "I noticed that you have found some young ladies for Bobby," he said. "That's good. You're going to do well on this tour." He told me that unlike Bobby, he preferred "mature" women. Pulling open the blinds in the bus lounge Bret pointed out a late thirty-something woman wearing a cowboy hat that could be seen from the bus, standing in the back-stage area. "That's *my* kind of woman," he confessed. He also indicated he didn't think his assistant would be as effective as me in procuring females and asked if I would bring the cowboy hat woman on board to meet him. So I guided the cowboy hat woman onto Bret's bus but by the time I did that, the two girls I had for Bobby apparently had grown impatient and disappeared. Bret was certainly smooth! There he was, telling me how he'd never stand in the way of me getting girls for Bobby while simultaneously cock-blocking my very efforts.

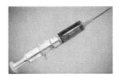

On another occasion in 2006, everyone in the organization except me was summoned for a tongue-lashing on Bret's bus. Poison had performed on August 15 at the Alltel Pavilion in Raleigh, North Carolina. Apparently at some point after the show, one of the girls from Bret's meet-and-greet was spotted on another band member's bus. On a Poison tour, world hunger is not as big an issue as a "tagged" chick being on the wrong bus. I remember this girl vividly. She made her way from one bus to the next all night long, looking for any action with any of the four Poison guys. Truth be told, I don't think she fucked any of them. It's actually rather amusing. Judging by the juvenile way they fight over girls, "pissing" on their "territo-ry," you'd think none of them had ever been laid before.

CHAPTER SEVEN

The next afternoon I heard Bret's voice over the security radio backstage at the Verizon Wireless Amphitheater in Charlotte, North Carolina, as I was getting out of the shower in Bobby's dressing room. He was obviously still pissed from the night before and everybody was being summoned. Janna Elias, Rob Stevenson, Mark Hogue, Kevin Carter — one by one Bret continued his roll call, yet I didn't hear *my* name. Brian Cocivera, Bob Huslinger, the list continued. Then, there was a long pause. "But I don't need Chris Long," Bret added. "I don't have any problems with Chris."

And it was true. Bret never had any "problems" with me. Maybe he took it easy on me because I always carried a notebook and wrote down everything I saw and heard. Maybe I'm endeared to him because I have his autograph tattooed on my right forearm. Maybe he just likes me. Whatever the reason might be, I'm probably the only one in the Poison organization who hasn't felt his wrath. In any case, I like Bret.

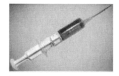

Then there is the biggest mystery surrounding Bret Michaels: The ever-present cowboy hat and bandana. Is he bald? Was he disfigured in an auto accident? Is he wearing a wig or a weave? Inquiring minds want to know. Unfortunately, I have no answer. Bobby told me in 2007 that not even members of his own band have seen Bret without some type of headgear since 1994. Personally, I don't see what the big deal is. Bret is a rock icon and a darn good lookin' fella. I'm sure he'd still be "hittin' it" regularly whether he had hair or not.

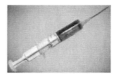

Master(s) of Disguise

By August 2006 Bobby developed an entire cast of backstage characters designed to amuse himself and irritate Bret. While in Florida, Bobby introduced two new alter egos. The one I named "Granddad" made a late night, after-show debut in the bus parking area behind The Times Forum in St. Petersburg. Bobby pulled his pajama pants up really high high and pulled his glasses down on his nose really low. He also combined goofy slippers with facial expressions similar to an elderly person with no teeth. The crew thought it was hilarious as did the throngs of fans who were still gathered at the backstage gate.

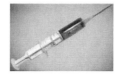

At the Sound Advice Amphitheater in West Palm Beach, Bobby appeared onstage for sound check as the "Big Pants Ninja." His make-up and costume looked as if he was from the cast of *Shogun*. Donned with a Japanese flag headband, oversized shorts and carrying a lunchbox, Bobby had everyone in stitches as he greeted stagehands using a Japanese accent.

That same day, Bobby instructed me to wear a ridiculously huge, multi-colored, velvet hat backstage all day until I changed into my security uniform around 7PM. The hat, best described as extremely "pimp-ish," drew backstage stares and laughter from the crew and fans. However, Rikki once again found little humor in my presentation. "What's up with the fucking hat, dude?" he asked me with dis-

gust as we sat in the catering room during dinner. But he was immediately more tolerant of the eyesore once I informed him that I was
wearing the hat per Bobby's request.

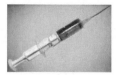

As the result of a bet made with Janna in 2006, Bobby introduced
us to "Tightie Whitey" shortly after breakfast, backstage at the
House of Blues in Myrtle Beach, South Carolina. Janna made a $20
bet with Bobby that he wouldn't go on Bret's bus wearing only
sneakers, white socks, white briefs and a white T-shirt. Bobby
accepted the terms of the bet and boarded Bret's bus as "Tightie
Whitey." According to Bobby, Bret was not particularly amused and
showed concern for Bobby's mental state.

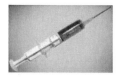

Bobby isn't the only band member who enjoys playing backstage
"dress up." In 2006, C.C. incorporated a concert security hat and
shirt with a short, dark wig and sunglasses to create his own alter
ego, the Gestapo-like veteran security guard character known as
Gordy Fein. As "Gordy," C.C. would accost fans gathered near the
backstage bus area. Shining a flashlight in their eyes, he would inter-

rogate fans, demanding proof of age and inquiring as to whether they'd been drinking or smoking pot. The funniest thing about Gordy in action was that C.C. was so convincing, fans had no clue they were being duped. I was once even approached by "Gordy." "Your association with the bass player is holding you back," he warned me.

Kevin Cater accompanying C.C. DeVille disguised as the legendary concert security guard Gordy Fein after the show in Charlotte, North Carolina on August 16, 2006.
(Photo courtesy of Kevin Carter)

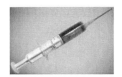

Y-M-C-A!

Bobby openly criticized Bret's new millennium "country boy" persona. He felt that Bret's ever-present cowboy hat made him look more like a member of the 1970s disco group, Village People, and less like an arena rock star. "When the hell did he become Southern?" Bobby once asked me. "He's from fucking Pennsylvania," he added with disgust. As the 2006 tour rolled on, Bobby was developing a sinister plan in which to publicly humiliate his countrified frontman.

Over the course of several weeks on the tour, Bobby began to acquire various props that for many people could be associated with, Village People. Inside his personal dressing room wardrobe case he somehow collected a construction worker's hat, a tool belt and believe it or not even an authentic Indian headdress. Bobby's plan was that at some point on the tour, while onstage during the band's signature ballad "Every Rose Has Its Thorn," the other three members of the band would appear onstage dressed as Village People members, mocking Bret's "cowboy" image in front of thousands of fans. After considerable preparation, the plot nearly came to fruition in Pennsylvania.

After performing in Hartford, Connecticut on Wednesday, August 9, Poison traveled through the night to Pittsburgh, Pennsylvania. The band would enjoy the next day off in Pittsburgh before performing on Friday, August 11 at the Post-Gazette Pavilion in Burgettstown, Pennsylvania. However, instead of remaining with the entourage following the Hartford show, Bret chose instead to fly home to Phoenix for his day off on Thursday and rejoin the tour in Pennsylvania on Friday.

Unfortunately there was a major international terrorist scare on Thursday, August 10. A plot to blow up planes in flight from the UK to the US had been foiled by Scotland Yard and airports in both countries were put on high alert. This created quite a challenge for getting Bret back to Pennsylvania for Poison's concert.

I remember receiving the call from Mark Hogue in my hotel room early in the morning of Friday, August 11. The news that I'd have to relay to Bobby wasn't good. Hogue informed me Bret had missed his flight out of Phoenix and a private jet would have to be chartered if he was going to arrive on time in Pennsylvania for that night's performance. Upon hearing this, Bobby became enraged. None of the other band members approved of Bret's diversion from the tour itinerary and now it would cost the band an astonishing $21,000 to charter a jet to ensure that Bret would be at the venue in time for that night's show.

But the issue was far from over. Bret's plane didn't land in Pennsylvania until after 5 PM. Given the Friday rush-hour/pre-concert traffic, it was feared that he still wouldn't arrive at the venue by show time. Consequently, arrangements were made for him to be transported by helicopter from the airport to the Post-Gazette Pavilion. Then there was the problem of getting Bret safely from the venue parking lot to the secured backstage area. As if things couldn't get any more complicated, he was taken from the helicopter and placed into a waiting SUV. Then, accompanied by a police escort, sirens and all, he was delivered to the doorstep of his tour bus where his local family members were throwing a backstage barbeque in his honor. The rock star had made one helluva entrance.

Come hell or high water, Bobby was going to see to it that Bret paid for his transgression. He instructed me to have the construction worker's outfit and Indian headdress ready for that night's show. Bobby also reasoned that given Rikki's typical onstage attire (cop hat, biker gear, etc.) he too already looked like a Village People member so it wasn't necessary for him to be part of the plot.

During Bret's onstage monologue leading into "Every Rose," Bobby cued me to discreetly deliver the props to the backstage area located directly behind Rikki's drum riser. The moment had finally arrived. But at the very last second, fearing that the joke would push Bret to quit the band, C.C. chickened out. As C.C. handed the headdress back to me, Bobby whipped off his construction worker's hat and instructed me to return the props to his dressing room. To my

knowledge the Village People prank was never resurrected, but the rivalry between Bobby and Bret was far from over.

Bret onstage in Pennsylvania on August 11, 2006.
Hey, that's me peeking out by Bret's left foot, between the stage and the barricade.
(Photo by Kevin Carter)

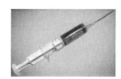

Here Comes Peter Cottontail

As a drummer myself, I've always admired the musicianship and showmanship of Rikki Rockett. In fact, to this day, even after working several tours and having interviewed him numerous times, I still have difficulty carrying on a conversation with the man without getting tongue-tied. And it's that obvious, giddy adulation that has compromised my ability to establish a legitimate personal or professional relationship with him. In fact, Bobby frequently mocks me, publicly referring to me as a "cock sucker" because of my admiration for his drummer. But truth be told, given my uncanny ability to always say the wrong thing in his presence, I think Rikki perceives me as an idiot.

Poison's 2006 tour rolled into New York's Jones Beach Amphitheater just in time to celebrate Rikki's forty-fifth birthday on August 8, 2006. Bobby wanted to make a big deal out of the occasion so he secretly made arrangements to surprise Rikki onstage that night with a huge sheet cake loaded with candles just before the band's encore. Calls were made that morning to some of Bobby's New York contacts and very stealth-like, the cake was delivered and concealed backstage at Jones Beach until show time. Desiring a very unique presentation while simultaneously annoying Bret, Bobby asked me two days earlier at New Jersey's PNC Center to arrange for

the cake to be brought onstage at Jones Beach by a girl in a bunny suit. I quietly mentioned Bobby's idea to Joe Cantaffa, a member of the PNC staff who coincidentally had a bunny suit. He also had a female friend named Jenny Eaton who would be available to make the trip to Jones Beach and was willing to wear the outfit onstage to present the cake.

Jenny Eaton as the "honey" bunny!
(Photo courtesy of Jenny Eaton)

Once I had confirmed that the bunny suit, the cake *and* Jenny were all backstage, Bobby instructed me to go on Bret's bus and give him a heads up concerning the cake presentation. To say the least, Bret was unenthused about the plan. "Why a bunny suit?" he asked me. "Wouldn't it be cooler if a couple of strippers brought the cake out? That's what Mötley Crüe would do."

I offered Bret no reply other than to suggest he take up his concerns directly with Bobby. I then returned to Bobby's bus where he was awaiting Bret's response. When I told him how unhappy Bret was with the plan, Bobby chuckled with delight.

Just before the band's encore, Bobby reminded Bret backstage about the cake. Dreading the humiliation of a girl coming onstage in a bunny suit, Bret acted surprised that the presentation was still happening. He suggested that the onstage celebration would be better suited in private. Bobby was undeterred by Bret's waffling and he quickly pushed me out onstage to lead the crowd of 5,000-plus fans in a rousing rendition of "Happy Birthday." Jenny brought the cake out (bunny suit and all) with candles blazing. The crowd got a charge out of the presentation, going crazy as Bobby attempted to smash the cake in Rikki's face while onstage.

Rikki Rockett's birthday celebration onstage at New York's Jones Beach Amphitheater on August 8, 2006. (Photo courtesy of Jenny Eaton)

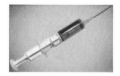

He Who Smelt It...

One of Bobby's most notorious (and often annoying) traits is his uncanny sense of smell. In fact, his sense is so sharp that it can actually be a curse to him as well as those who work and live around him. For years, I'd heard about Bob's "gift" but I didn't believe the hype until I officially started working for him in 2006.

Bobby once told me a tale about a disagreement he had with the landlord of an LA apartment he considered renting in the mid 1980s. The landlord insisted no pets had ever lived in that unit. Bobby (and his nose) begged to differ. He literally forced the landlord to smell the carpet on all fours until he finally admitted there had in fact been a dog living in the apartment at one time.

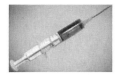

At every hotel where Poison stays, Bobby's room has to be inspected for unidentifiable and offensive odors before he can be brought in. If a cigarette had ever been smoked in a particular hotel room, Bobby would smell it and the room was deemed unacceptable. In New York during the 2006 tour Janna and I had to inspect four different rooms at the Long Island Marriott Hotel at 3AM before we found one suitable for Bobby.

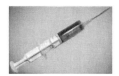

Most concert venue staff include local assistants called "runners." Runners run errands for the band and production staff. If a band member needed to leave the venue for any reason, a runner would either drive the band member to the desired location in the runner's personal vehicle or allow the band member to borrow the runner's vehicle. Before Bobby could get into a runner's car, the engine would have to be idling with the AC maxed and no hint of any kind of air freshener could be detected. If Bobby could smell anything, he'd get out of the car, refuse the ride and I'd be in trouble. In Myrtle Beach a runner grew so angry with Bobby's demands that he told me that Bobby could "fucking walk" to Starbucks for all he cared.

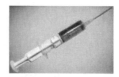

Everyone in the Poison organization is well aware of Bobby's acute olfactory sensitivities. I couldn't count the number of times that Bobby had to lay into Rikki's 2006 assistant Brian Cocivera for smoking around him. Even the opening acts were on notice. Despite the "No Smoking" signs posted nightly in plain view, members of the 2006 opening act, Cinderella still insisted on smoking in the back-stage area. That is until the LA show on July 1.

Cinderella's dressing room was directly across the hall from Bobby's and someone in their organization decided that morning to light up. When Bobby came down the hall a few minutes later the fragrance of cigarette smoke permeated the hallway. Bobby went ballistic! Seemingly out of control, he immediately plugged in his dressing room fan, ran it across the hall and blasted high-speed wind into Cinderella's dressing room. Emptying two cans of air freshener into the spinning blades, he declared, "No fucking smoking!" Within minutes, new signs were posted throughout the backstage area which now read, "No FUCKING Smoking!"

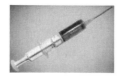

On July 8, 2006 Poison performed at the Verizon Wireless Amphitheater in San Antonio, Texas. Shortly after entering his dressing room Bobby informed me he suspected someone had been smoking pot in his dressing room bathroom. At this point I was really getting tired of the smell "thing." Nobody had been in his bathroom all day except me and Zak. He was obviously imagining things. There was no way he smelled any dope in that bathroom.

"Find Michael Grant," Bobby ordered. "Find out if he's been smoking dope with Zak in my bathroom." This was an absolutely absurd notion because as the frontman for the opening act Endeverafter, Grant was a consummate professional and had tremendous respect for Bobby. Zak was constantly hanging around Grant and the other Endeverafter band members, but frankly, I was surprised by Bobby's accusation.

"I get high all the time and I don't hide it," Grant confessed to me later in the day. But he eased my concerns by telling me that if he *was* going to get high, he certainly would have no need to light up in Bobby's dressing room and certainly not in Zak's presence.

Bobby remained so convinced of what he smelled that he began inspecting every square inch of his bathroom, searching for a clue. Then, he finally found it. Way up-high, laying on top of the paper towel dispenser was a tiny bit of a leftover joint. I was amazed. Korn, The Red Hot Chili Peppers and The Dave Matthews Band had all performed at that venue in the days leading up to Poison's appearance so it's anyone's guess who's dope it was. But I'd never doubt Bobby Dall's sense of smell again.

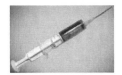

The biggest offender in this scenario are people who wear perfume and cologne. Many times, even close friends of Bobby's are denied access to him because of their strong perfume smell. Once, I had to deny R.V.'s girlfriend access to Bobby's tour bus because, as Bobby put it, "She smelled like a whore."

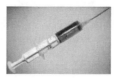

Bobby frequently accused C.C. of intentionally over spraying deodorant in Bobby's direction or near his dressing room out of spite. Come to think about it, I never heard C.C. ever deny the accusation either.

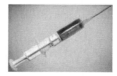

Once, while kissing his girlfriend, Bobby informed her he could smell tooth decay in one of her back molars and suggested she see a dentist. Insulted, the woman heeded Bobby's advice and sure enough, her dentist discovered an abscess. Yay, Dr. Bobby!

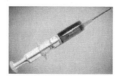

In 2007 Bobby insisted that he smelled something in the front of his tour bus. After weeks of complaining, his driver finally took apart the entire front interior of the bus and discovered a lost air freshener. Chalk up another one to "Toucan" Bob.

During a 2008 after-show dinner in Richmond, Virginia, Bobby once again noticed an offensive odor. He began frantically tearing through his dressing room until he found a little box of potpourri which had been placed behind the refrigerator. Right again, Bob!

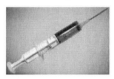

In 2009 Bobby sternly reprimanded one of his girlfriends for using scented laundry detergent. Upon arriving at his house he offered her a pair of his shorts and a T-shirt. He then ordered her to remove her clothes and put them in a bag and place the bag in his garage. He further informed the young woman that he'd prefer her to wipe fresh dog shit under his nose than to ever come to his house again after using that detergent. So smooth with the ladies, Bobby!

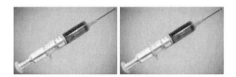

CHAPTER SEVEN

CHAPTER EIGHT

BLAME IT ON YOU - More ran-dumb behind-the-scenes crap

Poison's 2006 summer tour rolled on, creating an endless series of misadventures and near-catastrophes for all involved.

Instinctively, I knew that June 23, 2006 was going to be a bad day. Poison was performing a show that evening at 4 Bears Casino in New Town, North Dakota. It was an outdoor venue and when I walked off the bus at 8AM I discovered that once again, we were parked in the middle of a huge, sloppy mud pit. The day went downhill from there.

Fortunately, the casino offered the band courtesy hotel rooms for the day. After having checked in and showered, Bobby decided we would go downstairs to the hotel restaurant for a late lunch. He had been craving a cheeseburger like he'd seen the Endeverafter guys munching on earlier in the day. When we got to the restaurant we discovered that it didn't open for another five minutes. Bobby became furious because I hadn't verified that information before he came down. He thought being seen standing in the lobby for five minutes, talking to Michael Grant, waiting for the restaurant to open somehow made him look foolish. Once we got inside we discovered only the buffet line was open. This was definitely not what he had in mind. We then realized the burgers were only available at the concession stand located next to the restaurant in the hotel lobby. Unfortunately, all of the seats at the counter around the grille were taken so we couldn't place our order. Just like the episode at Applebee's back in Minnesota, Bobby snapped. This time, however, his frustrations were all directed at me.

"Goddamn it!" he screamed at the top of his voice in front of a restaurant full of people. "I can't take your incompetence anymore. One more fuck up and I'm sending you home!" He then stormed back upstairs to his room. I stayed downstairs to allow us both a chance to cool off.

Me and Zak with Endeverafter bassist Tommi Andrews in 2006.

Me with Endeverafter guitarist in Kristan MalloryCincinnati, Ohio.

For a rookie, I felt as if I was doing a decent job on the tour. Unfortunately Bobby doesn't remember the ninety-six things that a person gets right. He remembers the four things the person gets wrong. He then magnifies those wrongs by a factor of one hundred and you're forever perceived in his mind as being "incompetent." It wasn't fair and I'd had enough of being mocked, belittled and ridiculed. So I took a moment to breathe. I ordered lunch for Bobby and Zak and took the burgers back upstairs. I walked in Bobby's room and immediately announced that my bags were packed and I could be ready to leave in ten minutes.

"I've obviously become too much of a liability," I told Bobby and I suggested that I should fly home that night. Upon hearing this, Zak broke into tears — not so much because he was going to miss me, but because he feared that if I left the tour, Scotty Ludwick would be called in to replace me and there wasn't much love between Zak and

Scotty. But calmer heads prevailed. Realizing that I was dead serious, Bobby hugged me and apologized. By the time he finished his burger, all was (sorta) forgotten.

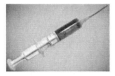

The Jersey Shore

I had a few interesting experiences in Atlantic City, New Jersey on August 13, 2006. The Poison concert was reportedly one of the first rock shows at the Wildwood Convention Center. The venue was located on the ocean so I went outside around noon to determine the best route for Bobby and I to take to get to the beach from the backstage area. Once outside I discovered every entrance to the venue was locked. So I had to walk around the entire building to get back to the bus area. The instant I walked through the backstage parking area entrance I was accosted by two venue security guards. Both guards appeared to be in their seventies and they were pissed. "Stop! Stop! You can't go through there!" they repeatedly shouted as they approached me. Finally realizing they were talking to me, I showed them my tour credentials. "I work for the band," I told them. But they could not have cared less. In fact, one of the guards threatened to have me arrested if I took another step further. "Arrest me?" I replied. "You're gonna have to fucking shoot me 'cuz I'll be dead if I don't get over to that tour bus in the next thirty seconds." So I went about my business as the guards continued their threats every step of the way. FYI - no arrests were made.

That night I committed perhaps the biggest offense of the tour — I accidentally brought the wrong girl to Bobby's dressing room after the show. There is a saying about someone being so mad they "spit nails." Well, that about describes Bobby's reaction when I entered his dressing room with the young woman whom he had "been" with in various other cities throughout the week. Although he calmly told the girl that he'd see her after his dinner, I could tell by the look in his eye that I had fucked up. Apparently he asked me to bring C.C.'s girlfriend Shannon Malone into his room to say "hello" — not the girl I brought back. Since I walked the girl past Shannon in the hallway, Bobby became worried that Shannon might rat him out to his girlfriend in Florida. I told Bobby before we left home for the tour that in case he got busted for having females around, three magic words would save him: "She's-with-Chris." In our hometown, I'm more famous than Bobby, so being romantically linked to beautiful women wasn't much of a stretch for me. However, by this time Bobby had so much contempt for me he would have rather been busted for cheating than suggest that any of his backstage "talent" had been with me.

Me and C.C. together backstage in Atlantic City on August 13, 2006 just before Bobby's blow-up.
(Photo by Kevin Carter)

In an attempt to fix the situation I quickly placed the girl in another room. When I returned to Bobby's dressing room I witnessed him freak out like never before. He was so angry the veins were bulging from his neck. He was spitting, stammering and was barely able to speak. As Bobby threw me out of his dressing room I saw Janna in the hallway. She had witnessed the entire incident. I shook her hand and told her good-bye because I was sure that I'd just been fired. However, Bobby soon calmed down and all was once again (sorta) forgotten.

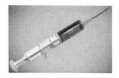

Hit it, C.C.

C.C. DeVille is without a doubt, one of the funniest, most articulate and well read people I've ever known. Despite his oddball public image, C.C. truly embodies someone who is "crazy like a fox." He'll sit and watch a football game and go on about how he knows nothing about sports while simultaneously firing off little-known NFL facts and stats on each team's players. For years, he's dumbed himself down in interviews, yet from politics to sports to the economy, the son of a bitch is up to date on everything. However, his boisterous personality often masked his street smarts.

> *"Everybody always talks about 'Rock.' If I were 'Roll,' I'd be pissed."*
>
> C.C. DeVille, June 2006

I never thought he received the musical credit and respect he deserved as a member of Poison, though. In fact, *Guitar World* magazine ranked C.C.'s solo performance on Poison's 1991 live record *Swallow This* at #1 on its all-time "100 Worst Guitar Solos" list, published in 2008.

Although his self-titled 2000 Samantha 7 solo record was overlooked by the masses, I thought it was heads and shoulders above anything he'd previously done. Clocking in at under thirty minutes, the eleven song collection of catchy, two and half minute, straight-to-the-hook earworms is quite possibly my all-time favorite rock record.

One afternoon while backstage, I noticed it sounded like a different drummer was playing at sound check. I walked onto the stage to discover C.C. behind Rikki's kit, playing better than any "real" drummer on the tour! Who knew?

We were together once at a Starbucks in Pittsburgh. Upon recognizing the animated- looking musician, the girl behind the counter

exclaimed, "I know you. You're Bret Michaels!" Visibly dejected, he quietly replied, "I ought to be."

It's funny because no matter how many times we met prior to 2006, C.C. never had a clue who I was. So I was really looking forward to establishing a friendship with him once I got on tour with Poison.

Me and C.C. backstage on August 3, 2002 in Poplar Bluff, MO. (Photo by Joe Deskin)

And we did become friends. Occasionally on tour he'd "borrow" me from Bobby and bring me over to his bus to prepare his after-show dinner. Though he's perfectly capable of feeding himself, it gave us a chance to hang out, listen to music and be pals.

But there's also a dark side to C.C. For reasons unknown to me, I think he feels like people are out to get him — as if he's the center of a conspiracy. Other times he can be downright mean. In Myrtle Beach, he became enraged when Kevin Carter couldn't find one of his guests in the crowd after Poison's show at the House of Blues. C.C. screamed at Kevin in front of a room full of people. As an off-

Me and C.C. backstage in Mankato, Minnesota
on the opening night of the 2006 tour.

duty North Carolina police offi-cer, Kevin was a real "tough guy." However, despite his toughness, Kevin was visibly upset by C.C.'s comments.

But I found C.C.'s quirky charm to be his most endearing quality. He once confessed to his girl-friend, "I love you more than snot, Shannon.

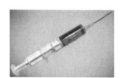

Writer's Block

During the first few weeks of the 2006 tour I tried to find spare time to write a feature story on the tour for *Brevard Live*. The story would coincide with Poison's August Florida concert dates. Unfortunately, there was no way Bobby was going to allow me to pursue any of my personal agendas on his watch — even if it did involve Poison. Consequently, despite actually being on the freaking tour, I had to submit to my editor, the worst, most rushed piece I had ever written on the band. I couldn't even get decent pictures. In fact, my submission was so weak I could only persuade my editor to give Poison a small photo on the cover of the issue as opposed to the usual full cover.

When copies of the issue made it out on the road, once again I looked, that's right, let's say it together, "incompetent." Bobby was furious over not having the cover and he placed the blame squarely on my shoulders. Of course, there was no way I could tell him he could have had the cover if he not been such a dick to me. Crew members also made disparaging comments to me about the article and C.C. even began referring to *Brevard Live* as "the little journal" I wrote for — ouch! The colleagues I wanted to impress most now all perceived me as a joke.

However, I did manage to get a couple of good one liners in the article, none of which amused Bobby. In the article I mentioned C.C. having a big penis. This actually ticked off Bobby for some reason. Earth to Bobby — it was a joke, dude. I also compared working for Bobby to slavery. I mentioned how I'd sing Negro spirituals daily as I hauled his luggage up and down flights of stairs. "I can't believe you said Negro spirituals," Bobby commented with disgust, peering at me over the top of his bifocals as he read the article. Conversely, C.C. loved the reference. Upon reading the article, he burst into Bobby's dressing room in uncontrollable laughter. "I can't believe you said Negro spirituals," he wailed. He then stood in the middle of Bobby's dressing room, gesturing as if he were picking cotton on a plantation. "Yasa, Masta Dall. Yasa!" he exclaimed while still laughing hysterically.

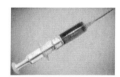

That Darn Tattoo!

Then there is the issue of what Bobby calls, "that darn tattoo." Although I've seen them at their best *and* their worst, I'll always be a Poison fan at heart. While hanging out with Bret during the Nashville after-show party on July 2, 2004, I asked him to sign my right forearm with a black Sharpie. I took great care all night not to smudge it. I even forfeited sex with a girl in my hotel room that night because I didn't want to break a sweat and smear the 2"x3" signature. In fact, I babied it all the way home the next day on the plane trip to Florida and during the hour-long drive from the airport to my house. I promptly booked an appointment at a local tattoo parlor and had it indelibly stamped. As a well-known entertainment personality on Florida's East Coast, I'm infamous for doing crazy shit. Sure I was a fan, but I also knew a stunt like this would certainly generate some extra attention. "That darn tattoo" became a great conversation

piece and chicks seem to dig it. However, I would *never* hear the end of it from Bobby and the other Poison members and crew. I also think Bret gets a kick out of knowing that *his* name is tattooed on the arm of *Bobby's* assistant.

C.C., Shannon and I at Niagara Falls on August 3, 2006. Look closely at my right forearm. It's a bird. It's a plane. No, it's "that darn tattoo." (Photo by Kevin Carter)

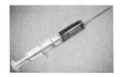

Boys Will Be Boys

Bobby, C.C. and I took a break one afternoon from The House of Blues in Myrtle Beach while the crew set up for that night's show. Due to insurance issues, HOB runners were not allowed to transport the talent off the corporate property. Instead, we had to wait (and wait) for a cab to arrive and whisk us off to the closest Starbucks coffee shop. As a hardcore coffee enthusiast, Bobby typically only patronized free-standing, or "proper" Starbucks stores. He found the staff at Starbucks stores located within other larger businesses to be "incompetent." And God help you if you messed up Bobby Dall's coffee order. Our cabbie, Erik, immediately took us to a Starbucks located in a local hotel lobby. Validating Bobby's Starbucks philosophy, the girl working the counter could barely speak English. We got back in the cab and Bobby once again informed Erik we needed a "proper" Starbucks location. He radioed his dispatcher for assistance. The woman taking his call (the cab company owner) informed us there was no difference in coffee shops and that we'd have to settle for where Erik took us. "We're the fucking customers!" I hollered from my shotgun position. Bobby then informed Erik that he needed to take us exactly where we told him. Getting no help from his dispatcher, Erik began calling fellow cab drivers on his cell phone for other Starbucks locations. When the dispatcher heard about this, she ordered Erik to drop us off immediately and return the cab. Outraged and insulted by this horrible service, C.C. asked Erik for a business card. Immediately he and Bobby began making prank calls to the dispatcher on their cell phones in the backseat. Within minutes, the two rock stars jammed the cab company with a dozen bogus cab requests.

Yes, with Erik's help, we finally found a "proper" Starbucks. Hooray! Bobby tipped Erik $100 for his effort.

It's ironic that Tropical Taxi boasts of offering "friendly" service.

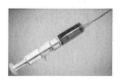

On August 5, 2006 Poison performed at The Tweeter Center, just outside of Boston. The dressing room area at the venue is set up much like a motel, in that the rooms have sliding glass doors which lead to a small patio. I walked around the back of Bobby's dressing room that afternoon and discovered him relaxing in a lounge chair, wearing sunglasses and soaking up the sunshine. He quietly and deviously instructed me to acquire a stack of "Bret" after-show passes for that night's show. Bret had one of his "hotties" flown in for a few days and seemed intent on impressing her. Completely aware of this, Bobby further instructed me to hand out "Bret" passes to as many fat girls in the crowd that night as possible. Bobby's goal was to embarrass Bret in front of his guest by having him completely surrounded by throngs of hideous-looking females after the show. It was a funny concept, however, I wasn't able to acquire enough "Bret" passes to make much of an impact.

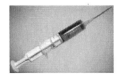

Considering that they were specifically built for live concerts, The Hard Rock in Orlando and The Joint in Las Vegas are the two most logistically challenging venues I've ever worked. In Orlando, artists must take an elevator to get from the dressing rooms down to the stage. This is fine, unless it's show time and the artist can't get to the stage because someone downstairs has the elevator jammed up. This happened to be the case when Poison played Orlando's Hard Rock on August 23, 2006.

Bobby and C.C. sitting at John Lennon's piano in the Orlando Hard Rock. (Photo by Kevin Carter)

135

Like every other night on the tour, Kevin Carter, Brian Cocivera and I began walking our "guys" from the dressing rooms to the stage as Poison's intro tape began to play. However, the elevator was already in use downstairs. The first and second verses of AC/DC's "Highway to Hell" had already played over the PA as we stood stranded on the second floor. Then, just when I didn't think the situation could get any more stressful, I saw Bret and Bob Huslinger walking towards the elevator, I've never witnessed Bret going onstage with the other band members. Typically he waits to go onstage until the last minute and this was the last minute. Finally, the elevator doors opened as the solo break from "Highway to Hell" began to play. Talk about an awkward moment. All four band members and all four assistants, all on one elevator and nobody was making eye contact with anybody. They've been through so much together for so many years, yet the tension was so thick you could cut it with a knife. The five second descent to the stage seemed like an eternity. The thought of a mechanical malfunction that would trap us all for any extended period was quite humorous to me at the time. Hell, it still is!

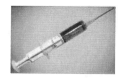

Another one of Bobby's pet peeves is Bret's lengthy onstage nightly monologues. In fact, this issue was such a thorn in Bobby's side during the 2006 tour that he bought a stopwatch to measure exactly how much time Bret wasted onstage with his nightly ramblings. FYI - in 2006 Bret devoted an average of seventeen minutes per show to in-between-song banter. It soon became an inside joke. Bobby began using the stopwatch to time EVERYTHING. If he asked someone a question, even if the answer was "yes" or "no," Bobby would time every response.

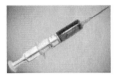

Don't Call Me Shirley

Oddly, I don't remember where this one took place. One night in 2006, while putting on his makeup prior to show time, Bobby looked in the mirror and commented on how he was beginning to resemble actress Shirley MacLaine as he aged. Rob Stevenson was in Bobby's dressing room at the time and we all found the comment rather amusing. Stevenson then began referring to Bobby as "the Shirley MacLaine of rock and roll" throughout the rest of the evening. As Poison went onstage that night, Stevenson went to the production office and located an online picture of Shirley MacLaine. He printed several black and white copies and created makeshift masks. When Bobby came side-stage the first time during the show he discovered several crew members wearing Shirley MacLaine masks. It was quite funny.

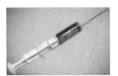

What Happens in Vegas…

My 2006 Las Vegas experience proved to be memorable on many levels. For starters, Bobby's girlfriend Meghan was out with us for a few days. Although I later heard reports that she, too, found me to be a bumbling, incompetent embarrassment to Bobby, I always liked Meghan and I was bummed when they broke up in 2007. However, the last thing I needed in Las Vegas was another "Dall" to attend to. We checked into The Hard Rock Hotel on our off-day on Monday,

July 3. Poison was performing the following night at The Joint, which is adjacent to the casino located within The Hard Rock Hotel. Once everybody from our entourage was settled in, we could basically stay put for two days. Getting settled in, however, would be no easy task.

Our busses were parked approximately one hundred yards from the hotel. I had to drag Bobby's cooler, Meghan's luggage, Bobby's luggage and Zak's luggage through the parking lot (in July), through the hotel, onto the elevator, and down a seemingly endless hallway. In the meantime, Bobby barked out additional orders via his cell phone from the comfort of his poolside cabana. "Are you shaving your legs? You take longer than a woman!" Bobby screamed on my voicemail as I frantically performed the near impossible one-man tasks. Whenever Meghan joined us on the road, Zak was bumped from Bobby's room to my room, so in Las Vegas I had to bring luggage to two different

Dall rooms. As I completed hauling everyone's personal effects to their respective rooms, Bobby called again to inform me that I needed to return to the bus and retrieve Meghan's makeup bag and Zak's belt. Hooray! Finally, by 3PM I was caught up and able to join our entourage poolside.

As winners of VH-1's "Roadie for a Day" contest, Missy Gilliam and Tara Perron were flown in from Maine for Poison's 2006 Las Vegas show. (Photo courtesy of Missy Gilliam)

Later that day I informed Bobby he'd been out of line with me and I didn't appreciate being constantly spoken to like I was an asshole. He was quick to reiterate that I was "incompetent" and "needed to get thicker skin."

A few days earlier in LA I prepared dinner on the bus for several of Bobby's after- show guests. I served the meals, poured and served drinks and then inquired whether anyone needed anything else. "No thanks," Bobby snapped. "Now get the fuck out!"

I had endured almost as much abuse as I could take from Bobby by the time we arrived in Las Vegas. However, I wasn't going to allow him to beat me down. I was going to finish the tour, even if it killed me. And it almost did. Within a few days I flew back to Florida after experiencing a physical and mental meltdown, a situation Bobby openly laughed about.

The Las Vegas experience didn't totally suck, though. On our off-night, Bobby, Meghan, C.C., and Shannon took in The Beatles tribute show on the strip while Zak and I were invited by Bobby's friends Ollie and Veronica to attend the Blue Man Group performance at The Venetian Hotel. Zak and I also took advantage of the opportunity to cruise the strip after the show.

I was with Rob Stevenson at the band's cabana on Tuesday morning July 4. Poison was set to perform that night and the band members wanted to enjoy every possible moment that day poolside, even Bret. As Stevenson and I prepared the cabana for the band's imminent arrival, I heard him say, "Hi, Paris." I looked up and there she was — Paris Hilton was standing right next to me as she made her way to the next cabana. Believe me, I have no hard-on for Paris

Hilton. However, she *is* a true show-biz icon. She was wearing her big signature sunglasses and was even carrying her little dog in a shoulder bag, just like I'd seen in magazines and on TV. It was completely surreal.

Bret enjoying a rare "out-of-bus" experience with VH-1 contest winner Tara Perron, poolside at The Hard Rock Hotel during Poison's 2006 tour.
(Photo courtesy of Tara Perron)

Of course Poison couldn't play Las Vegas without a little drama. Rikki nearly went to blows with the hotel chef over not being able to get a specific vegetarian meal. There was screaming, there was yelling and in short, it was an ugly scene.

As I've mentioned, The Joint is one of the two most logistically challenging venues I've worked. To get the band members from their rooms to the venue, you must endure endless hallways on various floors, through the kitchen area and past executive offices. Fans of the movie *This is Spinal Tap* will understand how confusing this was when I say "Hello, Cleveland!" Once the talent has made it to the backstage dressing rooms, they must then descend down a spiral staircase to the stage. To make matters more difficult you can only access the stage from stage right. I tried explaining to Bobby what he'd be dealing with that night before we left our hotel rooms, however he told me to "shut the fuck up" before I could finish. Consequently, I was stuck on the opposite side of the stage during the entire show. John Popplewell had to play bass tech *and* be Bobby's lapdog that night.

During one of his onstage Las Vegas monologues, Bret broke into an impromptu solo acoustic version of the Bob Dylan classic, "Knocking on Heaven's Door." Rikki quickly joined in and C.C. soon followed suit. Onstage, Bobby doesn't "jam." He plays only what has been rehearsed and "Knocking on Heaven's Door" had *not* been rehearsed. Furious over Bret's deviation from the nightly program, Bobby stormed off the stage following the show and immediately returned to his hotel room. Once Bobby and I returned to his room I could sense he really wasn't terribly upset. Apparently he was trying to make a point while stirring up some intra-band drama in the process.

Since Bobby hadn't returned to his dressing room after the show, I was sent back to retrieve a few of his belongings. On this night, the band members shared one dressing room. Upon returning upstairs I noticed Rob Stevenson standing in the hallway as I attempted to open the dressing room door. "Where are you going?" Stevenson asked me as he blocked the doorway. I informed him Bobby had sent me to retrieve a few of his things. "Okay," Stevenson conceded. "But I'm warning you, they're all in there and you're walking into a hornet's nest."

Attempting to be unobtrusive, I tiptoed into the dressing room and quietly reached for Bobby's shoes. Unfortunately, I was immediately busted. "Hey Chris," Bret shouted from the opposite side of the room. "What the fuck's wrong with Bobby?" he asked as he quickly cornered me. Luckily, I was able to convince him that all was well and Bobby only wanted to get back to his hotel room. Whether or not Bret actually bought my story is questionable, but he ended the dialogue and allowed me to finish my business. Bobby snickered with delight upon hearing of Bret's concern.

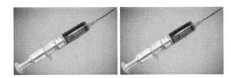

CHAPTER EIGHT

CHAPTER NINE

CRY TOUGH - A "mötley" Cinderella story

The most alluring aspect of working on Poison's 2006 tour was that Cinderella would be the opening act. Known for their string of signature 1980s arena rock anthems including "Shake Me" and "Gypsy Road," this raw, gusty, high-energy, blues-based band is without a doubt, my all-time favorite. It's too bad they probably think I'm a douche bag.

In 1995, my band Dead Serios opened for Cinderella on one of their Florida dates during the band's *Still Climbing* tour, and over the years I've conducted phoners with various members of the group for different publications. Being on the road with them on a sixty-two date tour was literally a dream come true. Unfortunately, my personal relationship with the band got off to a rocky start.

"I love the Cinderella guys. Onstage they're such a great rock band."

Bret Michaels, March 2002

One Saturday afternoon a few weeks prior to the Poison tour kick-off, I was out running local errands with Zak Dall. We were both excited about the upcoming tour, discussing all the fun we were going to have on the road that summer. At one point Zak mentioned to me that he had heard about an incident involving Poison and Mötley Crüe bassist Nikki Sixx. Zak was particularly troubled by the issue because he worshiped Nikki like Catholics worship the Virgin Mary.

Cinderella frontman Tom Keifer live onstage (Photo by Christine Herb)

The backstage area of the UMB Bank Pavilion in St. Louis is famous for its wall-to-wall display of live photos of the artists who have performed at the venue. The cool thing is that all of the pictures were taken while each artist was performing on the UMB stage. According to Zak, Nikki had reportedly removed a photo of Bret from the backstage wall and destroyed it when The Crüe performed at the UMB during their 2005 tour. Apparently it was going to be payback time when Poison performed at the same venue on June 16, 2006.

Within an hour of arriving at the venue, road manager Rob Stevenson spotted the backstage photo of Nikki and, in front of venue security, he climbed onto a chair, reached up and removed the photo of the Mötley Crüe founder. "This belongs to me now," Stevenson declared to the backstage guards.

The scene of the crime. Rob Stevenson leaves behind an empty space on the wall
where a photo of Nikki Sixx was once displayed backstage
at the UMB Bank Pavilion in St. Louis.

"Rock and roll is like primal instincts. It appeals to everybody."

Tom Keifer, March 2002

Later in the afternoon Zak approached me, visibly troubled with concerns that Stevenson was going to smash the photo. But that was the last I heard on the subject, until about an hour after that night's concert.

"Where's that fucking Nikki Sixx picture?" Stevenson screamed at me in Bobby's dressing room, shortly before the buses were scheduled to depart for the next day's show in Des Moines, Iowa.

Initially, I had no idea what he was talking about. But Stevenson was all too happy to quickly inform me that the photo was now missing. To say the least, he was extremely pissed about the situation. "Find Zak Dall," he bellowed. "If you find him, I'll bet you'll find my fucking picture!"

Me and Zak sightseeing in Green Bay, Wisconsin during Poison's 2006 tour.

Now *I* was the one stressed out. Zak was my buddy and if Stevenson found him before I did, Zak would be in serious trouble. Fortunately, I found Zak first. He was hanging out in the backstage parking area between his father's bus and Cinderella's bus. At first he denied any knowledge of the photo's whereabouts. After I carefully explained and emphasized the graveness of the situation, he finally came clean. "Wait here," he said as he turned and knocked on the door of Cinderella's bus. The door soon opened and Zak was ushered onboard. A minute later the door re-opened and Zak motioned for me to also come onto the bus.

I couldn't believe what was happening. Cinderella are my all-time rock and roll heroes. This was only the third show of the tour and

they were completely unaware of our previous connection. All I knew was that I had to confront my favorite band, face-to-face, on their own bus, over this stupid picture. Plus, at the time I was still wearing my lame-ass Poison security uniform. Hell, I even looked like a narc! But Zak was my pal and I'd do anything to keep him out of trouble

Me and Jeff LaBar backstage at LA's Universal Amphitheater in 2002

When I climbed aboard the bus I was immediately approached by guitarist Jeff LaBar. The Pennsylvania-born, take-no-shit musician was clearly not about to cop to anything, *especially* not to some stranger on his bus who was dressed like Barney Fife, the bumbling deputy sheriff on the popular 1960s sitcom, *The Andy Griffith Show*. "What's up?" he asked as he bowed up in my face. "We don't know anything about a picture," he maintained, as his bandmates and Zak observed.

Three shows into the tour and my worst tour fears were already coming true. Oh sure, I was hanging out with Cinderella, the holiest of all bands, but thanks to Zak, they now thought I was a dick!

"Look," I said as I desperately tried explaining my position. "I get the joke. It's really quite amusing, but I'm just trying to keep Zak out of trouble. And if that picture doesn't turn up soon, he's gonna be in BIG trouble!

Just then, LaBar's twenty-three-year-old wife Debby leaped up from the tour bus couch. "Alright, alright!" she muttered with disgust. "We were going to return it in a few days," she admitted as she

retrieved the picture from the back of the bus. "I'll even take the heat," she graciously offered. "I'm not afraid of Rob Stevenson."

Apparently earlier in the day, Zak heisted the picture from where Stevenson had stashed it backstage. He then gave it to the Cinderella guys for safe keeping.

Me and Cinderella's Fred Coury backstage in New York at Jones Beach on the 2006 tour (Photo by Kevin Carter)

"There is no doubt that people still want to be served rock and roll. It just hasn't been on the menu for the last ten years."

Tom Keifer, March 2002

Cinderella's Jeff LaBar and Eric Brittingham live onstage (Photo by Christine Herb)

Also concerned for Zak's welfare, Debby headed out with me to the venue's production offices with the now infamous framed photo in hand. Inside, we found Stevenson, still stewing over the situation.

"I heard you were looking for this," Debby told Stevenson as she returned the photo. "We were just playing a little gag. We were going to return it tomorrow," she bravely confessed.

"You went into my private area and took this from me?" Stevenson asked.

"Yes," Debby replied, taking full blame for the incident.

"Well, thank you very much," said Stevenson. "It took guts to fess up to this."

Things were now all good. The picture was returned, Debby took the heat and Zak was out of trouble, or so I thought. As I returned to Bobby's bus, I found Zak outside in tears.

Fred Coury live onstage (Photo by Christine Herb)

"They're going to smash it," Zak sobbed, clearly still distraught over the picture of his hero.

"That's the least of your worries," I tried to convince him. I conveyed that if he didn't pull himself together, Bobby would sense a problem and Zak would still be in trouble. I tried everything to get him to settle down. I tried telling him jokes — I even tried to get him to do jumping jacks — anything to get his mind off the fucking Nikki Sixx picture. However, unbeknownst to either of us, Bobby had been watching the entire event from the front window of his bus.

"Why the fuck is he crying?" Bobby demanded to know as he stormed off his bus.

"They're going to smash it," Zak muttered before I could further defuse the situation.

"You're still on that Nikki Sixx kick?" Bobby shouted, obviously having now run out of patience. Bobby passionately tried to articulate to Zak he should be more upset about what was done to "Uncle" Bret's picture and less concerned about Nikki's.

"Go to Hell, dad!" the teenager defiantly responded.

And with that, Zak found himself sailing through the air by the seat of his pants, flying onto the bus as Bobby scolded him along the way. The subsequent chewing out from dad was quite unpleasant to witness. As punishment for his outburst, Zak spent the next few days confined to the bus. No cell phone, no movies and no hanging out with Endeverafter. The poor kid was in Hell for the rest of the weekend. If he had only listened to his buddy, the "Rock Nanny," it would have saved him considerable grief and hardship!

The next day's show in Des Moines was an outdoor festival in an open field. It featured additional acts like Quiet Riot and Dokken. As I walked off Bobby's bus that morning I noticed LaBar and Cinderella bassist Eric Brittingham sitting at one of the outdoor backstage picnic tables. I took advantage of the opportunity to apologize for my previous night's intrusion and to formally introduce myself. I was relieved to have cleared the air with my heroes and they both had a good laugh when I confessed that I thought Cinderella was greater than The Rolling Stones.

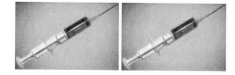

CHAPTER TEN

FLESH AND BLOOD - Injuries and ailments

Rikki Rockett once described the experience of touring as similar to being trapped in a bubble. Following my own touring experiences I found that to be an accurate analogy. On the road you're detached from the real world. You're never in one place long enough to feel like you're anyplace. Your every need is met while rarely having meaningful contact with any humans outside of the band's immediate entourage. However, this cozy isolation offers little shelter from the dangers of the outside world.

C.C. DeVille was the first casualty on the 2006 tour. Oddly, he was playing a little touch football with Bret behind the Rushmore Civic Center in Rapid City, South Dakota on June 25. He caught the ball incorrectly and jammed his middle finger. Screaming in pain, the guitarist was rushed to a local hospital. Bobby was getting a new bus that day so I was busy transferring food, luggage, and other personal effects from the old bus to the new one when I got the word of C.C.'s injury. Although no bones were broken, he had to wear a splint for the next week or two. Fortunately, C.C. still managed to perform and no shows were cancelled due to the mishap.

C.C. and Shannon on the way to the emergency room in Rapid City, South Dakota following C.C.'s football injury. (Photo by Kevin Carter)

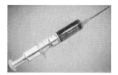

By the second week of the 2006 tour it seemed as if everyone from crew members to band members were getting sick. Somehow, I managed to dodge the bullet.

Throughout our little epidemic, Bret took the hardest hit. It was June 28 and he had been taken to the doctor on our day off. He had an extreme case of the flu and his doctor recommended cancelling the next night's show at the Tachi Palace, an Indian casino in Lemoore, California. However, Bret rose to the occasion and proved to be a consummate professional. Despite the ninety-plus degree onstage temperature, Bret braved his own elevated temperature and performed the show as scheduled. After the show I was asked to take a poster of the band to Bret's bus for him to sign for a local children's charity. Upon entering the bus, I found Bret lying on the couch in the front lounge. He was bundled in a heavy jacket and lying under a thick blanket, shivering as if it was winter. I showed him the poster and explained that his signature was needed. He was so weak he could barely sit up to sign his name. Throughout his illness and subsequent recovery, Bret never missed a show and he performed famously. A week later, it was Bobby's turn to catch the bug.

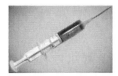

Bret had gotten word that Bobby had also fallen ill. From his bus, Bret radioed Bobby's dressing room indicating he still had some leftover flu meds. I was immediately dispatched to Bret's bus to pick up the goods. Bret led me to the back of his bus which was set up as a master bedroom. Bret dropped to his knees and pulled open a drawer located under his bed. The drawer was so tightly packed with what appeared to be an assortment of prescription drugs he could barely open or close it. He reached in the drawer and handed me a bottle of pills. "Oops. Those are the wrong ones," he said as he immediately snatched the bottle back and paused. "We wouldn't want to kill him — would we?" he deviously asked as he handed me the proper meds. Bret then wished Bobby a speedy recovery and I was sent on my way.

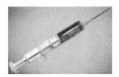

In 2006 I was probably the most notorious casualty of the tour. From the moment I accepted Bobby's offer to join the tour, he became a different guy. As I mentioned earlier, I initially interpreted his sudden nastiness, insults, belittling and mood swings as being pre-tour jitters. I was wrong. I carefully explained to Bobby before the tour that I could be his greatest asset if he dealt with me calmly. *Or*, hiring me *could* be the worst decision of his career if he chose to be a dick to me. He chose option "B."

Consequently his change in demeanor immediately caused my own pre-tour anxieties. I thought I was also dealing with temporary jitters and expected to settle down once we got on the road. Wrong again.

By the time I boarded the plane to leave for the tour on June 10, I was already suffering from a nervous stomach and frequent heart-burn. I'm no doctor and I don't want to offer medical misinforma-tion, but let's just say that after a month on the road I could barely function. In addition to my pre-tour symptoms, I was losing weight at an alarming rate, I was experiencing internal bleeding and by July 13, I could barely walk.

On tour there are people known as a "Rock Docs." These are local physicians known to the entertainment community in certain towns as medical professionals who will write untold prescriptions for tour-ing professionals without asking many (if any) questions. I had men-tioned my deteriorating condition to Bobby, but he just thought I was being a "whiner." After "whining" enough, a "Rock Doc" was called in to take a look at me backstage in Dallas on July 7. Dressed in a Harley-Davidson T-shirt and sporting a fine collection of tattoos, the Dallas doctor had me lie on a dressing room table. He poked me a few times in the stomach and determined me to be in good health. I'm sure if I needed a bottle of hydrocodone or oxycodone to get me through the pain of a hangnail, the good doctor could have hooked me up and everything would have been okay. Being in need of real treatment, this guy was of no value to me.

With my condition worsening, Rob Stevenson arranged for me to see a "real" doctor a few days later while the band was in Nashville on July 11. I appreciated Stevenson's concern for my health as he accompanied me to the doctor, even sitting in on my examination.

The Nashville doctor suspected I was dealing with a potentially serious condition and suggested that I leave the tour immediately and seek a specialist back home in Florida. I realized that was exactly what I needed, but I couldn't let Bobby win. I wouldn't let him beat me down. As I contemplated my next move, Stevenson and I took advantage of a day out from under Bobby's rule and enjoyed some sightseeing in Nashville before we returned to that night's venue. It was funny but the only times I was able to enjoy any significant sightseeing while on the 2006 tour was when Stevenson was transporting me to various medical facilities! It became clear to me in Cincinnati, Ohio on July 13 that I couldn't go on. Barely able to walk, I stumbled from the dressing room at the Riverbend Music Center to the bus. Within minutes, production manager Mark Hogue came on board to discover me shivering under a blanket. "This (tour) is all bullshit," he said. "All that matters is your health." Physically and emotionally I was spent. Hogue assured me that money would be no object. He further assured me the band would see to it that I received the best treatment and got back to work as quickly as possible. Upon returning to the venue with Stevenson after seeing a Cincinnati specialist, a flight was booked for me to return to Florida that night.

Despite Hogue's assurance that the band would take care of me, I overheard Bobby on the phone with his accountant in the production office cutting me from the band payroll before I could even leave for the airport. Since I began suffering symptoms prior to June 10, Bobby felt no obligation to continue paying me while sick at home. Furthermore, there was never any mention from the band regarding assistance in paying any of my medical expenses. As I struggled to prepare to leave, Bobby ordered me to bring his bags in from the bus and to "make it snappy." As I returned to the dressing room with his bags he confessed, "Now that you're leaving, I don't hate you!" As if he was enjoying my suffering, he joked with other members of the tour staff, stating that he had "killed another one!" He gleefully took credit for my condition but he wouldn't pay for my treatment. Later that afternoon Bobby, suggested in a conversation with Rikki Rockett that my illness was bogus and I was merely looking for an excuse to go home.

CHAPTER TEN

The earliest flight I could get to Florida didn't depart until after that night's show. In fact, it didn't depart until after all the buses, band and crew members had left the venue and were on the road to the next gig. That night I bid my good-byes to everyone on the tour staff. I was surprised when C.C. hugged me, kissed me and welled up as he asked me to recuperate and get back soon. Bret even joked about it, asking if he could have my condo bunk while I was gone.

In the immortal words of Twisted Sister, "You Can't Stop Rock and Roll." In the flash of an instant, I was a forgotten casualty. There I was — alone at 2AM, sitting on a curb, in the dark, in a now abandoned backstage parking area — with only a suitcase, watching the taillights of the tour buses and eighteen wheelers vanish into the night.

Fortunately my cab soon arrived to whisk me to the airport. I felt like shit, I looked like shit, and I didn't care. I was going home. In fact, upon returning home, my ex-girlfriend Karen commented that my weight loss and fatigued appearance made me almost unrecognizable.

I was immediately scheduled to undergo a colonoscopy (Google it for details) and I was diagnosed with colitis. In short, colitis is an inflammation of the colon. My doctor speculated that my condition was probably aggravated by job related stress. Hmm, what a shock. I got some rest, began a medication regimen and I was soon back on tour. I had to get back to work — I'd just racked up over $3,000 in uninsured medical expenses!

While I was away, Mark Hogue's assistant Karen Colvin called me nearly every day to check on my condition. Karen had been my guardian angel on the road and she helped me survive my first tour. We still remain close friends.

Upon rejoining the tour, I was picked up from the airport in Buffalo, New York on August 3 by my temporary replacement, Brian Young. Brian lived near Bobby's ski home in Salt Lake City, Utah. Given the fact that he was one of Bobby's closest friends, I had to chuckle when Brian looked at me, horrified when I got in the car and immediately asked, "Does he always yell about everything?" Wow, I guess everybody's "incompetent."

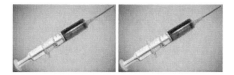

CHAPTER TEN

CHAPTER ELEVEN

POISON'D - In the studio 2007

In February 2007 I found myself at the world famous Henson Studios. Located in the heart of Hollywood, the facility was built by silent screen star Charlie Chaplin in the early 1900s and was originally a movie studio. In 1966 it was purchased, remodeled and transformed into the legendary A&M Studios by music moguls Herb Alpert and Jerry Moss. In 1999 the property was purchased by the Henson family. Jim Henson created *The Muppets*, one of TV's most successful kids shows. In May 2000 it officially re-opened as Henson Studios. During the A&M days, this was the facility where legendary artists like Carole King and The Carpenters recorded some of their biggest hits. As an admitted pop music nerd, it was hard to believe that I was so privileged as to be within such hallowed halls.

For the first time in thirteen years, Poison was in the studio recording a full-length record for a major label. Given the Top Twenty success of their 2006 "best of" collection, Capitol Records was once again behind Poison and ready to pony-up some cash. Unfortunately, the creative relationship between Bret and C.C. remained splintered. The label had its checkbook open, ready to give the band a second chance, but all they would ultimately deliver was a collection of newly recorded and re-released cover tunes.

CHAPTER ELEVEN

Bobby invited me to accompany Zak from Florida to visit him for
a few days in LA while he was working in the studio. Upon our
arrival at LAX, Zak and I took a cab to the Beverly Hills hotel where
Bobby and C.C. were staying. Zak and I were greeted by his father
and "Uncle" C.C. as we entered the hotel lobby. One of the songs
Poison considered recording for this new record, entitled *Poison'd*,
was Alice Cooper's 1976 ballad, "I Never Cry." As a huge Alice
Cooper fan, Bobby thought it was a great choice. But C.C. didn't
recall the song being a big enough hit for people to remember.
Known to the band as an expert in the field of pop music trivia, I was
questioned by Bobby and C.C. in the elevator on the way to our
rooms about the song's sales figures and final chart position. This
was a no-brainer. I, too, was a diehard Alice Cooper fan and I not
only recalled the record being a Top Twenty hit, but I also was able
to inform C.C. and Bobby that it appeared on Alice's 1976 album,
Goes to Hell (*Billboard* #27). C.C. remained skeptical. But after a little Internet research, Bobby verified my information. (Hmm. Maybe
I'm not so "incompetent" after all!)

Zak and I were staying in Bobby's room and after dropping off our
luggage, C.C., Bobby, Zak and I piled into Bobby's rental car. The
four of us journeyed to West Hollywood for a late night dinner with
Cinderella drummer Fred Coury at Frankie and Johnnie's New York
Pizza on Sunset Boulevard. It was great catching up with Fred, as I
hadn't seen him since the end of the 2006 tour. I thought he and I
were kinda becoming pals on the tour, however, after the LA trip he
no longer returned my calls.

Like countless times before, my role on this trip was that of "Rock
Nanny," attending to and entertaining now sixteen-year-old Zak.
Although we did enjoy some leisure time, shopping, sightseeing and
eating out, Bobby had a full workload. Consequently, most of our LA
time was spent in the studio. During the long *Poison'd* sessions, Zak
spent much of his time hanging out in the studio lounge, playing
video games and listening to music on his assortment of iGadgets.

These diversions afforded me extended nanny breaks, allowing me to hang out in the control room and experience the recording process first-hand. The record was being produced by Grammy Award-winning music biz guru Don Was. Don's impressive résumé includes producing critically acclaimed records for the likes of Bob Dylan, The Rolling Stones, Bonnie Raitt and Brian Wilson. For years, I had been paying my dues on an indie level, working in and learning my way around various recording studios from Florida to the Carolinas. So to actually be sitting at the mixing console, side-by-side with Don Was during a major label recording session made me awestruck to say the least.

I recall having dinner with Bobby one night in Florida prior to his leaving for the *Poison'd* sessions. He was excited about some of the fun, high-energy tunes the band planned on recording, such as a remake of the 1983 Van Halen classic, "Jump" and the 1973 Stealers Wheels hit, "Stuck in the Middle with You." So I was surprised and a bit disappointed to learn upon arriving at the studio that neither of these tunes would wind up on the record. In fact, *Poison'd* was now going to be filled with ridiculous, disconnected selections like The Marshall Tucker Band's "Can't You See." I realize Bret had been on a pseudo-cowboy kick in recent years, but I felt that VH-1's "All-Time #1 Hair Band" covering Southern rock was plain stupid. Maybe the track could've worked on one of Bret's solo records but it didn't work for Poison. I mean, c'mon. Does anyone really think C.C. DeVille or Rikki Rockett was ever even remotely influenced by Southern rock? Then there was perhaps the dopiest track, a remake of Justin Timberlake's 2006 dance hit, "Sexy Back." Not only was the choice completely misguided, but it sounded exactly like the original. I remember being in the studio while they were cutting the track and asking myself, "What the fuck are these guys doing?"

Poison'd was supposed to present an opportunity for the band to truly make a solid comeback. Capitol Records was enthusiastic enough about it that a top-name producer was brought in for the record and the band was given a budget to shoot a video for the track, "What I Like About You," originally recorded by The Romantics.

Even C.C. expressed excitement about the prospect of having a hit single as we listened to the playback of their remake of David Bowie's classic, "Suffragette City."

Poison session keyboardist Jimmy McGorman
(Photo courtesy of Amber Curtis)

I was in the studio with the band for several days. During that time they cut the basic tracks for what I thought was the record's crowning jewel — the aforementioned Alice Cooper hit, "I Never Cry." Because Bret rarely interacts with the other band members, I didn't see him the entire time I was in the studio. Hired-gun keyboardist Jimmy McGorman provided the guide vocals for the band to follow as they began recording the tune.

I've said it before and I'll say it again, Bobby Dall is a helluva player, far better than people give him credit for. In fact, I watched in amazement at the sound console with Don Was as Bobby nailed his bass parts for the track in a mere fifteen minutes. Rikki also cut his tracks for the tune within a couple of takes.

While Poison worked in Studio B, Guns N' Roses alumni Slash and Duff McKagan were in the adjacent studio recording *Libertad*, the sophomore record for their current project, Velvet Revolver. Zak is a huge rock and roll fan and can't get enough of the fast-paced lifestyle. He loves to be on tour with his dad and with his up-to-the-minute rock fashions, painted finger nails and expensive, ever-changing hair styles, it's often hard to tell between father and son who is the rock star. Standing in the hallway of Henson Studios and hearing Slash's signature guitar riffs buzzing through the walls was more than Zak could endure; he *had* to meet Slash. In fact, the prospect of meeting the rock icon was all I heard from Zak for days.

Then one night during one of Poison's sessions, Bobby finally gave in. He approached me with the official order, "Take Zak next door and introduce him to Slash."

This was the night of the 2007 Grammy Awards and Henson Studios was hosting a lavish after-show party. From current pop sensations like Christina Aguilera to retro hit makers like Taylor Dayne, the Henson party was an all-star event. Despite being Bobby Dall's son, getting Zak to Slash was going to be no easy feat.

I first introduced myself to one of Slash's handlers. I was quickly instructed to have Zak stand by for a few minutes while Slash finished his session. Before joining Guns N' Roses in the mid 1980s, Slash had actually auditioned for the guitar slot in Poison. Legend has it that Bret Michaels wanted Slash but was out voted by Bobby and Rikki who wanted C.C. DeVille. The possibility of lingering bad blood initially caused Bobby to be a bit skeptical about Zak meeting the guitar legend. But Slash couldn't have been nicer. Wearing black leather pants, a lavender silk shirt and his trademark top hat, he was

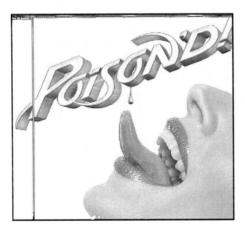

quite cordial and even displayed a sense of humor and patience when I had difficulty operating Zak's camera. Although the meeting was brief, Zak got to meet his hero and we quickly escaped the Grammy hoopla by slipping back into the quiet comfort of Studio B.

Sales of Poison's 2007 *Poison'd* record fell short of band members' expectations.

Band expectations were high. *Poison'd* could have been a great record and a huge commercial success. Initially, it was to include some terrific material. Instead, it featured an uninspiring song list without direction and it came nowhere close to being faithful to the band's true roots. Debuting at #32 on the *Billboard* charts, *Poison'd* sold approximately 21,000 units in its first week of release in June 2007. It vanished from the charts within a few weeks.

The following is my official *Poison'd* review as it appeared in July 2007 on the music Web site, Ink19.com. It may appear somewhat positive, but for me this was a scathing review. I wasn't sure how the band members were going to respond. But Bobby sent me an email saying that it was the best piece I had ever written about Poison and it was about time I "stopped kissing their asses."

POISON - *Poison'd* (EMI Music)

The newest passengers on the rapidly growing "Hey, let's release an album of cover tunes" bandwagon is none other than 1980s pop/metal poster boys, Poison. The band's current offering, simply titled Poison'd, features several newly recorded remakes of 1970s classics. Produced by legendary rock guru Don Was, it's rounded out by a fistful of previously released retreads from the band's infamous past.

Most music fans will agree that there is little appeal in an artist simply regurgitating what has already been done. Typically, what makes one of these types of records compelling is hearing a particular act put its own unique spin on a classic: transforming somebody else's tune into its own. However, in the case of Poison'd, the self-proclaimed Glam Slam Kings of Noise manage to get this basic concept completely ass-backward. They actually deliver their best versions of tunes on which they stick closest to the original recordings. Conversely, they run into trouble when they (God forbid) try to get creative.

At its best Poison'd offers raw, garage versions of The Sweet's "Little Willie," David Bowie's "Suffragette City," and Tom Petty's "I Need to Know" — classic gems with energy and attitude reminiscent of the band's earlier (and hungrier) Look What the Cat Dragged In era. However, the bastardized version of The Cars' "Just What I Needed" is sluggish and uninspired. And despite frontman Bret

Michaels' decade-long crusade trying to convince the world that he truly is "a little bit country and a little bit rock and roll," these high priests of Hair Metal should probably avoid covering Southern rock tunes in the future. In fact, their remake of The Marshall Tucker Band's "Can't You See" is certainly the record's square peg. But it could have been worse. At least they had enough sense to stay clear of Skynyrd and Hatchet!

While also sticking relatively true to the original version, the Poison'd version of The Romantics' "What I Like About You" is an album highlight. It comes across with a magical 1980s-something rock and roll party vibe. And it's their revival of Alice Cooper's 1976 hit ballad "I Never Cry" that could replace "Every Rose Has its Thorn" as Poison's best-known heartbreak ballad.

It ain't Dark Side of the Moon folks, but (thank God) it ain't Hollyweird either. Despite a few shortcomings, Poison'd still just might be the "feel good" record of the summer. —Christopher Long, Ink 19 (July 2007)

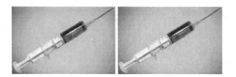

Rikki Rockett live onstage in 2007
(Photo by Christine Herb)

CHAPTER TWELVE

BACK TO THE ROCKING HORSE - The 2007 tour

After enduring the anxieties of working on the 2006 tour, I never again thought I'd find myself on the road with Poison. But like a painful tattoo, touring can be addictive...

It took quite a while to put my personal life back together following the 2006 tour. Initially I had hoped to continue working as Bobby's assistant after we returned home. Yet, considering all we had been through during the summer of 2006, there was no way we could maintain a formal working arrangement any longer. I found myself starting over professionally once I returned home. After being gone for months, my Florida nightclub gigs were all taken over by other DJs. As a result of my recently-acquired health condition, I had racked up thousands of dollars worth of medical bills on top of three weeks' worth of unpaid sick leave. Also during my time away, Katty, the female pop singer I was co-managing with former Kiss business manager C.K. Lendt, abandoned her solo career to pursue other interests. This, after we had invested two years and many thousands of dollars to develop her career. In short, I was now unemployed and nearly broke. Fortunately, by early 2007 I had re-established myself on Florida's entertainment scene, once again working fulltime as a nightclub personality.

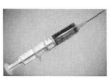

Immediately following the 2006 tour, I was contacted by Bret's longtime aide Janna Elias. Bret's solo career was starting to take off and she asked me to write a new bio for him. Given the recent bad blood between Bret and Bobby, Janna suggested that I keep the details of this arrangement confidential. I understood Janna's concerns and agreed to remain silent regarding her proposal. I didn't get to see much of Bret while on the road so I was thrilled to have the chance to maintain a post-tour connection with him. Janna further asked if I would offer the work gratis. Seeing this as a great opportunity to showcase my writing, I agreed to offer the piece free of charge. However, I never heard back from Bret's camp after submitting the bio. I sent several emails and left phone messages with Janna, yet my inquiries were ignored. In fact, despite working numerous dates on the next couple of tours, no mention was ever made regarding the 2006 bio. Consequently, I assumed Bret hated it and didn't want to hurt my feelings. Then, while conducting online research for this book in the summer of 2009, I solved the mystery. Not only was the bio acceptable, I discovered it was being used — a lot! I stumbled across Bret's Facebook page and to my surprise, he was using the bio I wrote. I soon took a look on Amazon.com to check the status of Bret's upcoming book and there it was again — of course, with no byline. I wasn't bothered by the lack of writer's credit. In the publicity world, writers are often un-credited on artist bios. I wasn't even upset about not getting paid, I offered my service free of charge as a personal favor. Given Bret's recent solo success, I realize his camp is busy frying bigger fish, but it was a bit hurtful being ignored.

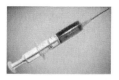

In early 2007 I was also performing with my new band The Glitter Döllz. This was a short-lived, pop rock act, fronted by eighteen-year-old singer Deana Lane. I met Deana backstage in Nashville, Tennessee while on the 2006 tour and we kept in touch after I returned home. Although she had zero band experience, she impressed me as being someone with a real desire to succeed. Jokingly, I told her I could easily put a band together for her if she moved to Florida. Less than a week later she was on my doorstep, ready to rock.

Although The Glitter Döllz didn't last long, it provided a great learning experience for Deana. I immediately began developing her as a solo artist. Bobby was so impressed with her early demos that he too became interested in her career. Even C.C. was excited about Deana's music. In fact, he physically dropped to his knees while backstage in Atlanta during the 2007 tour and literally begged her to allow him to play on one of her demos. And Rikki took to calling her "Cookie."

The Glitter Döllz: Me, Deana, Matt Rose, and Joe Del Corvo (Photo by Kevin Roberts)

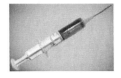

171

With his Melbourne house still being rented to his neighbor, Bobby spent much of 2006 and 2007 holed-up in a nearby luxury oceanside hotel room, organizing details for the upcoming *Poison'd* record and subsequent summer tour.

Although Bobby and I remained friends, in 2007 neither of us were comfortable with the prospect of reliving our previous tour experience. Consequently, I would play a considerably less prominent role on the 2007 tour than in 2006. The job of Bobby's assistant on or off tour is a near-impossible proposition for any one guy to handle. In 2007 Bobby began employing two tour assistants. R.V. returned to the Poison organization as Bobby's "lead dog" while my position was that of a sort of assistant-to-the-assistant, backing up R.V. on occasional tour stretches and selected dates. I was actually offered the gig as C.C.'s "guy" in 2007. Although I adore C.C., I was well aware of his dark side and I opted for the lesser position with Bobby.

Rikki Rockett live onstage on June 27, 2007 in Reading, Pennsylvania. (Photo by Christine Herb)

I connected with the tour on June 23 at The Blossom Music Center in Cuyahoga Falls, Ohio. Known for its all-wood construction band shell, The Blossom is a legendary facility and is one of my all-time favorite venues.

R.V.'s girlfriend Cindy happened to be in Cleveland that weekend and she picked me up from the airport and dropped me off at the venue. As I made my way backstage, I received a warm "welcome home" from various members of the crew whom I hadn't seen since the 2006 tour. Even Bret came off his bus to greet me. Referring to me as a "sexy bastard," Bret kissed me on the cheek and welcomed me back. He then made a smart-ass comment about Bobby needing two "guys."

Upon arriving in the backstage bus area I immediately recognized Bret's bus from the others. In fact, Stevie Wonder would have had a hard time missing it. Not only did one side of Bret's bus extend when parked, making it much larger than the others, but the entire side of the bus was plastered with a gigantic headshot of Bret to promote the premiere of his upcoming VH-1 reality show, *Rock of Love*. It was classic, over-the-top self-promotion and was fodder for considerable intra-band and crew jokes all summer.

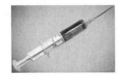

While R.V. attended to Bobby onstage during the shows in 2007, I hung out with Zak in the audience, cruising for chicks. One thing I noticed as we walked through the crowd each night was that despite the promotion behind the *Poison'd* record, audiences were still confused by the inclusion of cover tunes in Poison's set. In fact, some fans were downright angry and rightfully so. In addition to their 1988 Top Ten remake of Loggins and Messina's "Your Mama Don't Dance" and the lesser-known 2006 remake of Grand Funk Railroad's "We're an American Band," Poison's set now also featured *Poison'd* selections from the likes of The Marshall Tucker Band, Tom Petty and The Romantics. Sadly, in 2007 Poison had become a glorified cover band. I heard a guy in the men's room during one show screaming, "Why the fuck is Poison playing Tom Petty?" *Poison'd* was a mighty flop and by 2008 the band was back to performing their standard set list.

Bret performing a Florida solo gig in 2007.
(Photo by Christine Herb)

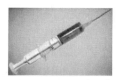

Once again I saw very little of Bret while working on the 2007 tour. We did, however, have one memorable experience — well, at least *I* remember it anyway.

Rewind to 2006. I met perhaps the most beautiful girl I'd ever seen. I spotted her as she walked through the gate at Poison's show in Hartford, Connecticut. She was slender, approximately one hundred-ten pounds (or less). She stood about five-foot-ten with green eyes, long blond hair and pristine perfect teeth. She was stunning. I i m m e d i a t e l y approached her and offered backstage passes to the girl and her friends. When Bobby entered his after-show meet-and-greet that night, he recognized the girl and

Bobby with friends during his after-show meet-and-greet in Columbus, Ohio on June 24, 2007. (Photo by Christopher Long)

told me her name was Lana. In recent years, Lana had been romantically connected to C.C. Bobby pulled Lana aside and warned her that C.C.'s current girlfriend, Shannon, was with him on the tour. But there was nothing to fear as Lana was totally cool. She hung out backstage briefly, said "hello" to a few old friends and went on her way, but not before giving me her phone number. Her number is *still* programmed in my phone!

When we arrived in Connecticut in 2007, I was eager to reconnect with Lana. I called her the day before Poison's June 26 concert at the Chevrolet Theater in Wallingford, Connecticut. Surprisingly, Lana remembered me and was thrilled by my offer of free tickets and after-show passes for the next night's show.

To my delight, Lana arrived at the concert dressed to kill. She was wearing the tiniest denim skirt I'd ever seen with a black tank top, black go-go boots and a black cowboy hat. Bret spotted Lana from the stage during the show and sent one of his guys into the crowd to "tag" her. During all of my experiences with Poison I'd only seen Bret in the dressing room area a couple of times, he was always on his bus. This night, however, Bret became so enraged upon discovering that Lana had already been "tagged" by me as a "Bobby" girl that he came storming through the backstage hallway and burst into Bobby's dressing room. I remained in the hall and a minute or two later Bret left Bobby's dressing room and again came storming toward me. He was still sweaty from the show and was huffing and puffing with rage. "Where's that tattoo, Chris Long?" Bret demanded to know as he scowled at me with the look of the devil in his eyes. He was obviously referring to the infamous tattoo on my right forearm of Bret's signature which I had gotten in 2004. Practically lifting me off the ground, he violently grabbed my arm and stuck it in the air for all to see. "Fuck you, Bob Dall! Fuck you!" he shouted as he allowed my arm to drop back to my side. And with that, he stormed off and headed toward his bus.

"Fuck you, Bob Dall! Fuck you!"

Bret Michaels, June 2007

The funny thing was there was no need for Bret to get so worked up. Bobby and Lana were genuinely just friends. She came to Bobby's dressing room with her guests after the show. They hung out for a few minutes and that was it. Lana was always cool.

Miss Lana created quite a commotion backstage in Connecticut on the 2007 tour. (Photo courtesy of Lana Ivan)

Bobby Dall live onstage in 2007.
(Photo by Christine Herb)

"My band has become splintered."

Rikki Rockett, September 2003

C.C. DeVille onstage at New York's Jones Beach
Amphitheater in 2004 (Photo by Jennifer Berman)

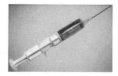

One of the opening acts in 2007 was Ratt, a hard rock band from LA that enjoyed chart success and heavy MTV play in the 1980s with such hits as "Round and Round," "Lay it Down" and "Way Cool Jr." Despite their legendary status, the Ratt guys seemed to exude a sort of negative energy. I had previous experiences with original members, guitarist Warren DeMartini, drummer Bobby Blotzer and hired-gun guitarist John Corabi. None struck me as being particularly pleasant individuals. Although longtime bassist Robbie Crane always seemed upbeat, frontman Stephen Pearcy always appeared (to me) to be pissed off. In short, I steered clear of Ratt in 2007.

Ratt guitarist Warren DeMartini
(Photo by Christine Herb)

Ratt frontman Stephen Pearcy
(Photo by Christine Herb)

I wasn't the only one who sensed problems within Ratt's camp in 2007. I was standing in the hallway with Bobby backstage following Ratt's August 30 performance at the Crown Coliseum in

Fayetteville, North Carolina. As the band came off the stage, some members went to their dressing rooms in one direction, other members went in an opposite direction, and Blotzer marched off to the band's bus. "I'm smelling some tension," Bobby hollered sarcastically as various Ratt members passed by, prompting one crew member to comment that Ratt was a "miserable bunch."

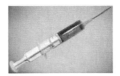

One of the tour's openers in 2007 were the Swedish sleaze rock upstarts, Vains of Jenna, throwbacks to the 1980s Sunset Strip-style of rock and roll. They also recorded for Filthy Note Records, owned by multimedia personality Bam Margera. I recall Bam coming to the June 27 show in Reading, Pennsylvania. The entire backstage was all abuzz in anticipation of Bam's arrival. Everyone from backstage tag-alongs to band members lined up to have their picture taken with the skateboarding, daredevil celebrity whose television credits included the MTV reality shows, *Jackass*, *Viva La Bam* and *Bam's Unholy Union*. Upon entering the backstage green room, Bam threw his keys

to R.V. and asked him to move his car into the designated VIP parking area. Of course, I had to check out Bam's ride, so I accompanied R.V. on his mission. Oh yeah — it was a sweet, late model, black Mercedes.

Bam Margera onstage with Poison during the June 27, 2007 show in Reading, Pennsylvania.
(Photo by Christine Herb)

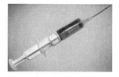

After two years of planning, Bobby's pet project came to fruition on August 2, 2007 when Poison's St. Louis performance was recorded for a spectacular, high definition home DVD release. Ultimately titled *Live, Raw and Uncut*, the package included a DVD, a bonus live audio CD and a full-color booklet. Sold exclusively at Best Buy stores, the DVD would reach the Top Ten on the *Billboard* home video chart in 2008.

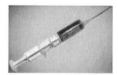

C.C. DeVille live in West Palm Beach, Florida in 2007. (Photo by Christine Herb)

In addition to the excitement of the new record and the success of the subsequent tour, 2007 was also a big year on a personal level for C.C. and longtime girlfriend Shannon Malone. On March 15 they welcomed into the world their first-born child, a son named Vallon DeVille Johannesson. I remember meeting Vallon when Shannon first brought him out during the 2007 tour. That little guy was not only adorable, but he was one of the most well-behaved babies I've ever seen.

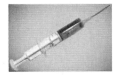

Poison rounded out an exciting year when they performed live in October on the roof of the Best Buy store in LA as part of the super-hyped *Guitar Hero III* video game premiere party.

Rikki Rockett live in 2007. (Photo by Christine Herb)

By the close of 2007, Poison was riding high. It seemed as if nothing, not even a record full of crappy cover tunes, could slow their current momentum. Well, almost nothing…

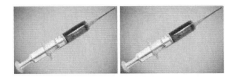

CHAPTER TWELVE

CHAPTER THIRTEEN

LIVE, RAW AND UNCUT - The 2008 tour

"Don't say a fucking word to anybody about this," R.V. commanded, in a phone conversation with me on Tuesday, March 25. "Rockett got popped for rape at LAX," R.V. continued. His words shot through me like a bullet. Was this some kind of a joke? Unfortunately, R.V. was dead serious.

2008 was a banner year for Poison. In March the band performed abroad for the first time in more than a decade, performing with Kiss in Wellington, New Zealand. In July they staged another highly successful US summer concert tour. The forty-nine city outing featured special guests Don Dokken and Sebastian Bach. It was also an exciting year for the band's individual members. January marked the second season kick-off of Bret's popular VH-1 reality series *Rock of Love*. Bobby entertained offers to manage various up-and-coming acts, C.C. was adjusting to fatherhood and Rikki married his longtime girlfriend Melanie Martel in LA on October 18. All was well in Poison's world in 2008 except for one ugly detail.

On Monday, March 24 the members of Poison were returning to the US following their performance in New Zealand. As they passed through customs at LAX, the L.A.P.D. was standing by, waiting for Rikki.

On September 23, 2007, a man representing himself as Rikki

Rockett allegedly raped a woman in a hotel room at the Silver Star Casino in Neshoba County, Mississippi. A warrant was subsequently issued and now, six months later, Rikki was arrested. I immediately knew the charge was bogus. To me, Rikki had always been an extremely honorable guy. Not only that, he hadn't even been in Mississippi since Poison played there in July 2007. And on the day in question he was actually with his fiancée, shopping for a wedding dress. However, Rikki was in serious trouble. Despite his airtight alibi, high-priced attorneys and big time management, the issue was not going away. Rikki's entire future hung in the balance, along with the future of Poison.

"They wanted to prosecute me. They wanted blood."

Rikki Rockett, June 2008

In June I was preparing a Poison cover story for *Brevard Live* that would coincide with the band's upcoming Florida concert appearances. I wanted to include quotes from all four band members. Given the dark cloud that had been hanging over Rikki for several weeks I thought I'd give him an opportunity to talk about something other than his legal drama. By then, however, the authorities discovered Rikki was in fact, the wrong guy. Cops were now looking for 48-year-old John Minskoff. Reportedly, Minskoff had a history of passing himself off as a rock musician in order to pick up women. As of this writing, a warrant is still out for his arrest. Now officially exonerated on all charges, Rikki understandably wanted to talk at great length about the case during our interview and take full advantage of another opportunity to clear his name.

"Our justice system is extremely broken."

Rikki Rockett, June 2008

"It's really a crazy, stupid story," Rikki commented as he began to recount his recent real-life nightmare. After spending a day in jail, Rikki was placed under house arrest. "I couldn't leave the house without being followed," he added. I asked why the authorities had continued to build a case against him despite his rock solid alibi. "They wanted to prosecute me. They wanted blood," he replied.

Featuring my Poison cover story, the July 2008 issue of *Brevard Live*
was the most popular of the year.

To say the least, the media had a field day covering Rikki's plight. Certain "journalists" even seemed to take great pleasure in pronouncing him guilty as charged before he even had a chance to make his case. In response to Rikki being released on bond, a pinhead blogging for the Web site bittenandbound.com wrote: "It looks like the singer may have skated away, for now." The douche bag who wrote the "report" didn't know enough about the subject to know Rikki was the drummer, not the band's singer, yet was certain of Rikki's guilt. On March 31, 2008 an unnamed journalist for the Web site thesuperficial.com offered this ridiculous commentary: "Did he do it? Oh yeah. I mean look at the guy. Not exactly a pussy magnet." Wow, what journalistic integrity.

"It's not freedom of the press, it's freedom of harassment."

Rikki Rockett, June 2008

"Maybe she wasn't raped at all," Rikki speculated. "Maybe she had an affair with this guy, I don't know. Whatever happened between them — I wasn't part of it. Personally, I don't think she was raped. I think she got caught with her pants down."

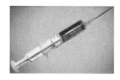

A few years earlier in 2006, Rikki launched a custom drum company called Chop Shop with business partner Brian Cocivera. After personal disputes with Cocivera, Rikki formed his own company in 2007, Rockett Drum Works. As a longtime drummer, even my off-the-rack kits were always customized in some way. With Rikki now completely running the show, I had to have one of his unique, one-of-a-kind kits. I asked him to create an outrageously eye-catching kit for me. He soon emailed me a photo of a single drum prototype for a camouflage-finish kit. But instead of the typical military-style green and brown camouflage, Rikki's version of camouflage incorporated shades of pink. I couldn't have been more thrilled with the concept. In fact, one of my DJ aliases is "Mr. Pink." Unfortunately I'd recently had a personal business venture fall through. Although I lost a small fortune, nothing was going to keep me from owning my dream kit. Little by little, month by month, I made payments to Rikki's company. I may have appeared for a while to be an unreliable dick in the eyes of my hero, but I paid off those babies in full. In the spring of 2008, the UPS man finally made the long-awaited delivery.

Rikki designed and created my custom, hot pink camouflage kit in 2008.
(Photo by Kevin Roberts)

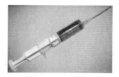

Prior to the 2008 tour kick-off, Bobby and I continued working with Deana Lane, the singer I brought in from Tennessee. Although she lived with me and I was financially supporting her and funding her career, Bobby mentored the young singer/songwriter and offered her considerable professional guidance. Unfortunately, after two years of hard work, dedication and $15,000 worth of (my) development capital, Deana determined Bobby and I were unfit to represent her. Consequently, she returned to Tennessee to go on her own. She soon referred to her Florida experience as being "lame," and characterized the two individuals she had worked with in Florida as a "junkie" and a "liar." Hmm, I wonder whom she was talking about.

Bobby and I spent considerable time working
with Deana Lane in 2007 and 2008.
(Photo by Kevin Roberts)

Bobby clowning around at Deana's
2008 photo shoot in
Melbourne, Florida.
(Photo by Kevin Roberts)

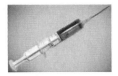

The 2008 tour kicked off on July 3 in Salt Lake City, Utah. In 2006, Bobby's friend Brian Young filled in for me while I was on sick leave. In 2007 Brian became C.C.'s "guy." In 2008 he replaced R.V. as Bobby's fulltime guy while I continued my role as an assistant-to-the-assistant on random dates.

I first hooked up with the tour in Tampa on July 22. Since he lives in Florida, Bobby is besieged by family, friends and wannabes the moment both sides of his ass cross the Sunshine State line. Anybody who's ever even waited on him at his hometown McDonald's becomes Bobby's best friend when Poison comes to Florida. In fact, during the 2006 tour, Bobby's personal guest list in West Palm Beach exceeded two hundred. Despite his penchant for being difficult at times, the fact is that Bobby goes out of his way to accommodate his family and friends when on tour, especially in Florida. The guy does his very best to ensure that every one of his guests are taken care of properly. In my view, his generosity goes largely unappreciated. Florida concert dates are stress-filled experiences for Bobby. In return for his efforts, the poor guy gets bitched at by family and friends over such issues as seat locations or the level of their pass status. Sadly, Bobby is rarely ever thanked for his generosity and I wanted to make sure I was available to assist him for both 2008 Florida concert dates.

A huge hospitality tent was set up backstage in West Palm Beach to accommodate Bobby's after-show guests. Despite being a sort of hometown show, this was one of the nights when Bobby wasn't up to seeing anyone after the concert. He did want to see a couple of friends who worked at his local Starbucks shop. I went to the VIP tent, found his three friends and brought them to Bobby, backstage in a now empty and quiet catering room. In the middle of the conversation Bobby jumped up from the table. "I gotta show you something!"

he exclaimed. He sprinted to the bus and moments later returned to the catering room and immediately slapped a recent issue of *The Palm Beach Post* on the table at which we were sitting. The paper was opened to the entertainment section. Accompanying a major feature promoting Poison's West Palm Beach show was a huge photo of Bobby plastered across half of the page. Grinning ear to ear, Bobby was so proud to have finally received Bret-like press exposure. Also, after seeing my face grace the front pages of our hometown publications for so long, he was more giddy about trumping me and he told me so. "Now that's *real* press!" he boasted to his friends as he shoved the paper in my face.

C.C. DeVille and Bobby Dall onstage at Riverbend Amphitheater in Cincinnati, Ohio on August 16, 2008. (Photos by Evan Taylor Roach)

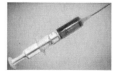

To maintain their privacy while on tour, Poison members use aliases when checking into hotels. In 2008 Bobby's alias was Barack

Obama. I still can't figure out how he thought he'd enjoy anonymity by using the name of somebody a million times more famous than himself. Surprisingly, several hotel staff members on the tour actually believed the presumptive Democratic nominee for President of the United States was staying at their hotel in the same group as other such distinguished colleagues as Dick Hurts and Heywood Jablowme. In an attempt to further tease gullible hotel employees, Bobby purchased a life-size, cardboard stand-up of Obama to place in his hotel room each night.

I remember the morning of August 12. We were staying at the Hilton in Iselin, New Jersey. Since we wouldn't be leaving to go to the venue for several hours, Bobby ordered breakfast from room service. It seemingly took forever for his meal to arrive. Finally there was a knock at the door. I opened the door to discover several staff members in the hall. I immediately thought it was odd that four or five people were required to bring up one small breakfast cart. "Is he here?" asked a petite, twenty-something black woman who was part of the group delivering the meal. At first I had no idea what she was talking about. "I just wanted to ask him to sign this," she added, as she held up a copy of Obama's 2006 book *The Audacity of Hope*. It then dawned on me. She thought Bobby was Barack Obama! Overhearing the conversation from inside his room, Bobby came to the door and laughingly informed the woman that she had been duped. Despite his efforts to console her, she was visibly disappointed. Bobby offered to sign the book himself, but an autograph from an aging 1980s Hair Metal dude was hardly consolation to this young Obama fan.

This life-size, cardboard stand-up of Barack Obama was the source of considerable amusement on the 2008 tour.

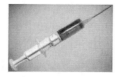

Just like my previous Poison tour experiences, I saw little of newly-minted reality TV star, Bret Michaels. In fact, I probably only spoke to Bret once in 2008. I noticed him throwing the football around with Big John in the outdoor backstage area prior to the August 13 show in Richmond, Virginia. Unlike the warm welcome I received in 2007, in 2008 Bret acted as if we were strangers. Hardly even looking at me, Bret said "hello" as he continued tossing the ball back and forth with Big John. After he repeated his predictable snide comment about Bobby needing two "guys," I told him I'd see him later. With the exception of live performances, that was the last I saw of Bret in 2008.

I discovered this tribute to Bret hanging from inside the backstage fence when I came off the bus in Noblesville, Indiana on Friday morning, August 15. (Photo courtesy of Karen Colvin)

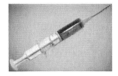

I remember first meeting the soon-to-be Mrs. Rikki Rockett, singer/songwriter Melanie Martel. The couple met at one of her live performances in Nashville during the 2006 tour. I remember seeing them having breakfast in the hotel restaurant one morning shortly after they got together and thinking how absolutely stunning Melanie was. Despite working on the tour in 2006, Melanie never seemed to remember me. In 2007 we saw a lot of each other while Poison was in the studio and still she had no idea who I was. I said "hello" to Melanie one night backstage during the 2007 tour and once again I had to remind her that I was one of Bobby's "guys" for the last two tours and that we had hung out in LA during the *Poison'd* sessions. Then one night in 2008 the unthinkable happened — Melanie Martel finally recognized me. I was walking through the backstage parking area after the show at the PNC Arts Center in Homdel, New Jersey. I was headed toward Bobby's bus, and noticed Melanie standing out-side Rikki's bus. I politely said "hello" as I passed her when all of sudden she called my name. Stunned, I stopped and turned around as she motioned me to come back. "Weren't you in the band Dead Serios?" she asked. Holy cow! Not only did the beauty finally know my name, she knew my band. I walked back towards Rikki's bus and we began chatting. I soon learned that Melanie was also originally from Florida. Although she was thirteen years younger than me, as a kid she used to come see my band's all-ages concerts. Dead Serios was an outrageous, hard rocking band. Apparently, we were unfor-gettable too. After hanging around her for three years, it took the Dead Serios connection for her to notice me. Hilarious! Even Bobby got a kick out of that one.

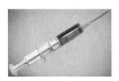

Bret devotes much of his time on tour to orchestrating his solo career. Rikki spends his offstage tour time shopping, working on video projects and riding his motorcycle, which is transported city-to-city in a covered trailer, hitched to the back of his tour bus. For Bobby, with the exception of his daily Starbucks visits, it's all business at all times. He has two primary interests in life: Poison, and making money. In fact, there is rarely a time when he's not near a TV tuned to CNN, keeping up on current events and stock market reports. On the bus — CNN. In the dressing room — CNN. Even when he's in the hotel gym working out, he's in front of a TV tuned

to CNN. That's why you'd better bring a sharp "blade" if you intend to have a battle of wits with Bobby Dall. Despite never graduating from high school, he's a political, financial and business know-it-all. And I'm not even close to joking.

I snapped this one of Rikki and Brian Cocivera from the tour bus window while en route from the hotel to Nashville's Starwood Amphitheater in July 2006.

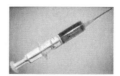

One night following a show on the 2008 tour, Bobby called for me from the back of the bus. He was lying on his bed, watching TV and he asked me to join him. Okay, relax - this story is only going to be half as gay as what you're thinking. As we were lying on the bed, watching CNN and chatting about world affairs, Bobby mentioned that he needed me to help him stay on his medication schedule. He then dumped the contents of his travel bag on the bed. The assorted collection of prescription meds that poured out from his bag resembled a kid emptying a trick-or-treat sack at Halloween. Realizing that I always carried a notebook (and always took notes), Bobby began dictating to me his daily drug regimen as I wrote it all down. He then asked for my assistance in helping him stick to the schedule, a request I did my best to honor.

Bobby backstage in Cleveland on August 14 with one of Poison's all-time biggest fans, Lydia Puccini. (Photo courtesy of Lydia Puccini)

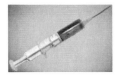

As for C.C., we shared several nights staying up late during the 2008 tour passionately discussing current events as well as various aspects of fatherhood.

Early in the tour C.C. fired his current "guy." When I first hooked up with the band in Florida for a couple of days on July 22, Bobby approached me about joining the tour full-time as C.C.'s new assistant. I told Bobby that I needed to first go home for a night and get a few personal affairs in order. Upon returning the following day I was informed that after careful consideration, C.C. determined that he liked me too much to put me through the anxieties of working for him. Consequently, he chose tour veteran Geno Aldridge to complete the tour, thus allowing me to reprise my usual role as Bobby's back-up "guy," working random tour dates through out 2008.

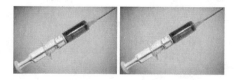

CHAPTER FOURTEEN

POWER TO THE PEOPLE - The Fans

The connection between performer and fan is and always has been a very personal one. While most Poison fans are content with simply buying the group's music, coming to the shows and having a good time, some fans innocently seek guitar picks, drum sticks or autographs from the various band members. Others feel they are somehow entitled to even more. Shamelessly, they often go to great lengths to attain a personal one-on-one experience with their favorite member of their favorite band.

Early in my relationship with Poison I noticed that certain members of the band harbored contempt for their fans. Bobby and C.C. dread the nightly after-show meet-and-greets to such an extent that by 2006 C.C. rarely met any fans unless they were paying for the privilege at an organized post-concert event. In their defense, however, I can say Poison's attitude toward their fans isn't as odd, cold or callous as it may seem. In fact, it's quite common in the rock world.

Years ago, Kiss recognized the substantial dollar value attached to the meet-and-greet experience. In 2003 they began selling premium concert packages which typically included "ringside" seats, T-shirts and a pre-show photo opportunity with the band. Typically these "experiences" cost dedicated fans between $500 and $1,000 each.

In 2006 Aerosmith also sold these types of concert packages. I took Zak to see the Aerosmith/Mötley Crüe show at the Sound Advice Amphitheater in West Palm Beach, Florida on November 24, 2006. As VIPs, Zak and I were allowed to enter a private pre- show meet-and-greet with Aerosmith being held for their Japanese fans. While standing in the meet-and-greet line, an excited female Japanese fan told me (in broken English) that she had paid $5,000 for the privilege.

Once Zak and I got to the front of the line I recognized the stressed look on their assistant's face as he began interrogating us with the same questions I asked when interrogating Poison's after-show guests. He wanted to know who we were, why we were there and who was our contact. I also noticed some of Aerosmith's members didn't seem any more enthusiastic about meeting their fans than Poison's members were about meeting their own. I definitely recognized the pained look on drummer Joey Kramer's face as he stood at the meet-and-greet, posing for picture after picture. As I leaned toward Joe Perry to inform him that Zak's dad was Bobby Dall, it became clear to me that he couldn't have cared less. However, I must say that in stark contrast to his fellow bandmates, frontman Steven Tyler was charming, outgoing and at least *seemed* to enjoy meeting everyone who came through the line. Having gone through the tour experience myself, I could now relate to any band's lack of enthusiasm regarding fans.

In 2008 Poison got into the game by offering *their* fans deluxe concert packages. This included an 8x10 promo photo autographed by all four band members, a personal band "experience" and a tour of one of the band member's buses.

Despite his frequent grumbling about dealing with people, Bobby was typically the one Poison member who made the time each night to meet these fans, pose for pictures and even offered his private bus for the nightly fan tours. Following the 2008 show at Cincinnati's

Riverbend Amphitheater, Bobby asked Rob Stevenson to line up the premium ticket buyers outside his dressing room door. When they least expected, Bobby leaped through the doorway like a silly monster and yelled, "Boogety!" Shaking hands and taking pictures with fans while laughing and smiling, Bobby personally greeted each person in line — and seemed to enjoy it. Now that was a unique band experience. In fact, I rarely saw him in such a jovial post-show mood.

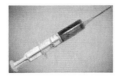

In director Martin Scorsese's 1983 film *The King of Comedy*, Robert De Niro stars as Rupert Pupkin, a fan obsessed with onscreen TV talk show host Jerry Langford, played by veteran comedian Jerry Lewis. Pupkin becomes so delusional about a non-existent relationship with Langford that he breaks into the talk show host's onscreen home, fantasizing he is an invited guest. Ultimately, Pupkin tries to further connect with Langford by kidnapping him. After working on several Poison tours I learned that the fanatical behavior portrayed in *The King of Comedy* wasn't terribly uncommon.

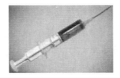

Bobby prepped me on various fan issues prior to the 2006 tour, but I thought he was being over dramatic. After all, the 1980s were long over and although Poison was still filling arenas and amphitheaters, they hadn't had a Top Ten record in years. So I naïvely thought his concerns were unwarranted. However, I soon discovered that I had a lot to learn about Poison and their fans.

Something strange that I immediately noticed while working my first Poison tour is that some of their more fanatical followers actually conduct themselves as if they personally know the band. Fans even learn the names of the members' children. While walking Zak through crowds at his father's concerts, people would often shout his name. Being just a kid, Zak would often ask me whether or not he really knew the people who seemed to know him.

 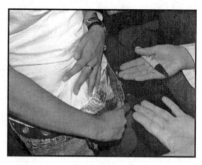

In 2006 this gal asked C.C. to autograph her breast. This actually is a common request. (Photo by Kevin Carter)

This young woman asked C.C. to autograph her panties during a 2006 meet-and-greet in Utah. That's completely normal — right? (Photo by Kevin Carter)

Although most of these overzealous fans certainly don't know the band on any professional or personal level, they often know just enough about a particular member to con an outsider. However, you can't bullshit an actual band member. When confronted by one of these fans, Bobby will directly set the person straight if he doesn't really know them. In an effort to be polite, sometimes the other Poison members are actually nice to these folks but try to get away from them as quickly as possible. Unfortunately, playing nice can often further encourage certain fans.

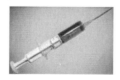

Creepy!

The band and crew were relaxing, enjoying a little quiet time off one night during the 2006 tour. Our entourage was staying at The Embassy Suites Hotel in Raleigh, North Carolina on Monday, August 14. Bobby and I had just returned from having dinner across the street at P.F. Chang's when we ran into C.C. and Kevin Carter in the hotel lobby. As the four of us stood in the lobby making plans to watch Monday Night Football, I noticed a guy trying to get C.C.'s attention. C.C. was rather cordial toward him so I didn't think much of it and after a brief dialogue, the guy went on his way. Unbeknownst to us, the guy was watching as C.C. returned to his room. He spotted C.C.'s room number and called him about an hour later while C.C. was taking a nap. Understandably unhappy about being disturbed, C.C. told the guy not bother him. Within minutes the guy was outside C.C.'s room, sliding a letter under the door. Although I didn't personally read the note, it was reportedly creepy enough that Kevin Carter and Rob Stevenson had to have the guy removed from the hotel property by local police.

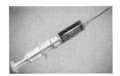

Rikki spotted a true diehard fan in the crowd during the Richmond, Virginia show in 2008. Rikki was so taken aback by the guy's enthusiasm during the show that he invited the fan and his girlfriend to hang out on his bus afterward. Fans often ask for souvenirs like drum sticks and guitar picks. This fan, however, had the nerve to ask Rikki for his shoes! "Are you fucking serious?" Rikki asked. The guy admitted he was dead serious as his girlfriend urged him to shut up. Rikki then suggested that the guy should get off his bus before he left with the shoe up his ass!

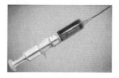

I was working the 2007 show in Reading, Pennsylvania. A female friend of mine from Orlando who just happened to be at the Reading show gave her extra after-show "Bobby" pass to a young diehard female Bobby fan who was seated next to her. After the show I brought the young woman to the room where Bobby would soon conduct his meet-and-greet. The well-mannered, petite blond quietly and patiently waited for her rock and roll hero. Over the years I've witnessed many ardent fans meeting Poison members, but when Bobby approached this particular girl, she went absolutely ballistic! She began wailing hysterically as Bobby gave her an autograph. Placing both hands on the girl's shoulders, Bobby gently sat her down as I gave her a bottled water. With tears running down her face she continued to sob as she confessed her love for Bobby. He then invited her to hang out. But before he could finish signing his last few autographs the young woman mysteriously vanished. That was the last we ever heard from her.

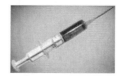

I was approached by a woman in the lobby of the New England Dodge Amphitheater in Hartford, Connecticut on August 9, 2006. Dressed in my police-style security uniform, I was easily spotted by fans as I walked through the crowd, "tagging" babes for Bobby prior to each night's show. She frantically informed me she was a member of Bret's fan club and her after-show passes were not at the box office as promised. Visibly upset, she showed me her fan club credentials. She was in fact a fan club member and had apparently bought her own tickets. As Bobby's "guy" I was never involved in Bret's affairs. However, since we gave away after-show passes like

Halloween candy every night I didn't see the harm in accommodating the woman. Consequently, I put Bret's "guy's" initials on two passes to indicate which meet-and-greet they were to attend. To my chagrin, the woman and her boyfriend wound up in Bobby's after-show group. Bobby hated having to meet more than a few people each night so I certainly didn't need two more. As he worked his way around the room, meeting fans and signing autographs, I noticed the woman inching toward Bobby. Little by little, she got closer and closer. She then leaped from the crowd, trying to tackle him with a

bear hug. "What the fuck?" Bobby shouted as we both tried to fight off the deranged fan. Visibly shaken by the incident, Bobby immediately returned to his dressing room as the woman was removed from the premises. "That's it," he announced. "I'm done for the night!"

Bobby signing autographs backstage in Hartford moments before being attacked by a crazed fan. (Photo by Sandy Creamer)

The more tenacious and fervent fans know no limits when it comes to tracking down the band while on tour. I found it astounding that we could check into a hotel, in the middle of nowhere, on a day off, hundreds of miles from the next show and still discover fans camped out in the lobby in anticipation of Poison's arrival. Often, we would check into a hotel in the morning on a day off and not check out until sound check the next afternoon. This created an opportunity for the band to become "sitting ducks" for almost two days. Although the band members use aliases when staying at hotels, they easily remain some of the most recognizable figures in rock and roll. Once C.C. DeVille is spotted in a hotel lobby, word travels fast amongst dedicated followers. I've seen fans camped out in hotel lobbies for days waiting to get a glimpse of, or an autograph from, their favorite band member. In Alabama while on the 2006 tour, several fans actually followed me and Bobby from the hotel lobby through the adjacent shopping mall carrying armloads of Poison memorabilia they wanted signed. Once cornered in the mall's Starbucks coffee shop, Bobby graciously signed their stuff.

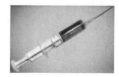

We were staying at a hotel in Albuquerque, New Mexico in 2006. It was an off day between shows in Las Vegas and Oklahoma City, however, locals somehow knew the band was in town. R.V. was out with us for a few days and he and Bobby took Zak to the movies shortly after checking into our rooms. I stayed at the hotel to catch up on some personal business. Realizing we were out of frozen treats for that night, I called a cab to take me to the local supermarket. I quickly discovered that even the cabbie knew Poison was staying at the hotel. "Is Mr. Rikki Rockett here?" the cabbie inquired. With five tour buses parked outside the hotel there was no point in lying to the guy so I concurred that "Mr. Rikki Rockett" was in fact staying at the hotel. The cabbie then went into great detail explaining how he loved Rikki and that he was his favorite Poison member. He further confessed that he was a singer and he wanted to audition as a backup vocalist for Poison. Then he proceeded to serenade me with a medley of Poison's biggest hits... all the way to the supermarket. Honestly, he was more funny than he was creepy. In fact, I got a real kick out of my singing cabbie.

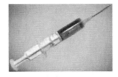

I met a couple early one morning in the lobby of the Radisson Hotel in Green Bay, Wisconsin during the 2006 tour. We checked in the day before so the band members were all settled and sound asleep in their rooms. Due to my many responsibilities as Bobby's "guy," I had to be up early every morning. As I walked through the hotel in pursuit of a morning newspaper and a cup of coffee, I noticed a guy and a girl quietly sitting in the lobby. I suspected they were Poison fans who were camping out. I was in a particularly good mood and the girl was a total cutie so I approached the couple and said "hello." The nerdish-looking guy appeared to be in his late twenties. He introduced himself as Joe and his girlfriend as Lucille. Lucille was an attractive, petite, brunette who looked to be about twenty-five. My instincts were correct. They were Poison fans — at least Joe was. Actually, not only was he a Poison fan, he was a *super* Poison fan. Joe was quick to confess that Poison was his favorite band and he eagerly shared with me the story of how he was sent to the principal's office in the first grade for bringing a Poison record to school for Show and Tell.

Sensing that the couple wasn't really "together" I made a playful advance towards Lucille, which was a shitty thing to do because Joe seemed like a sweetheart. However, neither made any attempt to discourage my flirtatious approach. Jokingly, I suggested that Lucille should accompany me to my room while I located backstage passes for the couple to that night's show. I was shocked when Joe appeared to be cool with my proposition. Lucille didn't object either. I couldn't believe it. I had just met this couple ten minutes earlier and the guy was ready to surrender his girlfriend to me for a couple of after-show passes. But I couldn't press the issue any further. They were both nice people and I didn't want to be generating that kind of karma. Ultimately, I took care of them with no strings attached.

205

Damn my conscience.

I continued to set Joe up with tickets and passes for subsequent Poison shows throughout the summer of 2006. When, I returned to Florida for a few days during the tour and wasn't always able to extend him the personal VIP treatment he was now accustomed to receiving, it created a big problem for me.

I awoke to the sound of my cell phone ringing at 7AM, on Saturday July 15. Joe was on the line. He informed me he was already at the venue for that night's show and was curious as to when he could pick up his tickets and passes from the box office. "Are you kidding me?" I asked. Annoyed by this early morning intrusion, I quickly explained that I was hundreds of miles away and couldn't do much for him. I further explained that tickets and passes aren't brought to the box office until approximately 5PM. I suggested that he try to relax and have a nice day. By 2PM my phone rang again. It was Joe. He was concerned because that night's venue was an open field at a Nebraska fairgrounds and he wasn't sure where to go for the after-show meet-and-greet. "Joe, I'm hundreds of miles away," I reminded him again. "Just relax and figure it out." Joe called several more times throughout the afternoon with similar concerns. By 11PM Joe was getting on my nerves. The show was over and he was panicking because no one had come to take him to that night's makeshift out-door backstage area. Now I was pissed. "Joe, I'm hundreds of miles away." I reminded him yet again. "There's nothing I can do." I did try on Joe's behalf to contact several members of Poison's tour staff, however my calls were going unanswered. At midnight I had the same conversation with Joe. And again at 1AM. "Go home, Joe!" I instructed as I reminded him once more, "I'm hundreds of miles away. There's nothing I can do."But I've met lots of "Joes" over the years. That's why it's difficult to be nice to fans on the road. You try to be cool and hook someone up and it bites you in the ass every time.

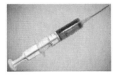

Seriously, Folks!

I must admit that despite some derisive comments made by the band members, Poison really does try to be fan friendly. However, some people are never satisfied no matter how much they're given. In 2008 C.C. and I discussed how demanding fans had become in recent years. I've seen complete strangers approach Poison members and demand free tickets, as if they were owed something. Once they get free tickets, then they want after-show passes. Then they get pissed if band members don't kiss their asses at the meet-and-greet. "When I was a kid, I was grateful just to go to a show," C.C. once recalled to me. "The idea of going backstage never even crossed my mind."

Bret discussing quantum physics with a special friend backstage in 2007

In 2006 Bobby was contacted by an ex-girlfriend who wanted to attend the show in Oklahoma City. Bobby graciously offered free tickets and backstage passes to the girl and her family. She then had the balls to ask him for additional tickets and passes for TWENTY-FOUR of her friends. That ain't a misprint. The girl asked Bobby for a grand total of twenty-seven FREE tickets — and she wasn't even fucking him anymore! The craziest part of the story is Bobby generously honored the request. He did, however, draw the line the following night when the same girl came to the Dallas show. As I was preparing Bobby to go onstage she actually called me on my cell phone, requesting that I deliver cold beers to her and her parents whom Bobby had placed in the front row. Bobby immediately called her back and informed the girl that I worked for him, not her.

(Photo by Sandy Creamer)
(Photo by Karen Madsen)(above)
(Photo by Leslie Emmetts) (left)

Not all Poison fans are "creepy." In fact, in the 2000s, many of their teenage fans were quite cool.

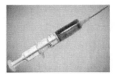

In 2006 I met a couple of girls backstage in Chicago who were best friends. We immediately connected and I saw to it that they received VIP treatment at every Poison show they attended that summer. I kept in touch with them after the tour and developed a personal friendship with one. In 2007 and 2008, I continued to set them up with tickets and passes, even during tour stretches I wasn't working. For three tours they received up front seats at any Poison show they wanted to attend, after-show passes and they even enjoyed a few intimate experiences with various band members. Wow! What fan could ask for more? They could.

"It's the 'NASCAR' in us that gets us in trouble."

Bobby Dall, August 2008

Once again, I made arrangements for my Chicago girls to receive the royal treatment at a Poison show a few days before I joined the tour in 2008. I was at home in Florida watching movies with my teenage son late one night when my cell phone rang. On the line was my gal pal from Chicago. Apparently she was outraged over how she'd been treated at that night's show. I asked if she'd gotten the tickets. She had. I asked if they were good seats. They were. She had a thing for Bobby and was angry because he was tied up that night with other after-show business and wasn't seeing *anybody*. "I've never been so insulted!" she screamed at me over the phone. I told her not to take it personally. In fact, Bret has actually kept his own father held up for hours waiting backstage for a private moment with his son. This was of little solace to the girl who after years of VIP treatment, vowed never to attend another Poison show.

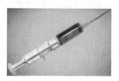

In 2007 I met two twenty-year-old girls named Tiffany and Jasmine while working the show in Denver. I brought them backstage because they seemed like fun and they indicated they wanted to "do" each other in front of Bobby. Unfortunately, as he came off his bus to meet them, Bobby spotted the girls coming off another bus. Bobby always abided by the "bro road code" and never "tapped" any girls who had been with his other band members. So at least for that tour, the bi-cuties were off limits. However, I hooked the girls up with free tickets and passes for subsequent Poison shows that summer and stayed in touch with Tiffany after the tour. For a while she seemed like a cool chick. Then one day in 2008 she called me asking me to hook her up with tickets for Mötley Crüe's upcoming show in Denver. I explained that I didn't work for Mötley, but as a favor I'd make a few calls. I mentioned the situation to R.V. and he contacted his buddy Tony who worked for Mötley's drummer Tommy Lee. Tony asked to see pictures of the girls. I emailed pics to R.V. who then forwarded them to Tony. Tony declined to take care of the girls because he didn't think they measured up to Tommy's standards. I didn't want to hurt their feelings so I merely confessed to Tiffany that I couldn't come through for them. She then informed me that I had "fucked her over" and I would "owe her big time" when Poison came to Denver a few weeks later.

Despite being put off by her arrogance and rudeness, I still wanted to see her get naked with Jasmine so I hooked them up with tickets and passes for Poison's 2008 show. I mentioned the girls to Bobby on the afternoon of the show and he seemed interested in seeing them later that night. Unfortunately, after confirming this with the girls, Bobby received an unexpected visit from one of his established hotties, hence negating the arrangements made with Tiffany and Jasmine. Once again not wanting to insult the girls, I still brought them backstage after the show in hopes of hooking them up with an alternative band member. Like I've said, things get really chaotic backstage for an hour or so following a show. As a personal assistant, the last thing I have time for is impatient groupies trying to claw their way backstage. Within seconds of the show finale, my two impatient bi-cuties were bombarding me with text messages before I could even get Bobby to his dressing room.

"Stand by," I texted Tiffany.

"What the fuck?" she quickly responded. "We're tired of standing by."

I don't know which is more insulting — being condescended to by a "ten" because she knows she's hot enough to get away with it, or by a "six" who *thinks* she's a "ten."

Consequently, none of the band members were seeing anyone that night. My two bi-cuties were treated to free tickets and after-show passes. They had pictures taken with opening act frontman Sebastian Bach and got to briefly say "hello" to Rikki. Wow, I guess I had "fucked them over" again.

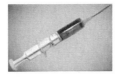

Condom-nation

I was approached backstage by a woman in 2006 I recognized from the hotel bar the night before. She introduced me to her eighteen-year-old friend whom I also recognized from the previous evening. I was told that the eighteen-year-old was a "Bobby Girl," which is tour-speak for a female whose sole purpose for being backstage was to "be" with Bobby Dall. I was further informed that the eighteen-year-old was a virgin and she'd saved her virginity for Bobby. I confronted the teen about this and she concurred. After checking her ID to verify her age, I sprinted down the hallway from the catering room to Bobby's dressing room. Half out of breath, I burst through the doorway and announced, "Boss, you're not gonna believe this one!" Bobby was skeptical about my information, but he agreed to see the girl after the show.

I brought the girl to Bobby's dressing room following the show and he also asked to see her ID. Upon Bobby verifying the girl's age, I was immediately asked to stand guard outside the dressing room door so they could get better acquainted without interruption. Lighting director Fi-Fi Miller saw me standing guard as he walked passed Bobby's dressing room and burst into hysterical laughter. No words needed to be exchanged. Fi-Fi was a touring veteran and knew exactly what was going on. I don't know for certain what happened between Bobby and his teenage admirer that night, but at one point the door opened ever so slightly and through the crack Bobby asked me to quickly bring him a condom. Perhaps he was showing his young guest balloon tricks.

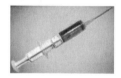

While working the 2008 tour I was with Bobby backstage following Poison's August 12 show in Holmdel, New Jersey. The dressing rooms at the PNC Amphitheater are located underground and give the feeling of being in a dungeon. The other band members chose to live in their respective buses that day instead of utilizing their designated dressing rooms. Consequently, the backstage post-show silence was deafening.

As Bobby and I sat quietly discussing that night's show, a stunning five-foot-ten woman in her early thirties with long, straight blond hair, wearing a short skirt, heels and a cowboy hat sashayed into Bobby's dressing room as if she owned the place. Like somebody who had done this many times before, she approached Bobby, introduced herself as Shelby and made her herself at home. Taking a seat next to Bobby she shared a fabulous tale of how she "accidentally" made it through security and down two flights of stairs, ultimately winding up in Bobby's dressing room by mistake. Although her story was certainly compelling, the girl was obviously a pro. By now I knew the drill so I stood up, excused myself and went into the hallway to stand guard (again) while Bobby and his new friend "visited." Once again, I spotted Fi-Fi coming down the hallway headed to Bobby's dressing room in his nightly pursuit of a cold Red Bull. Noticing me standing guard he shrugged his shoulders, snickered and kept walking. A few minutes later I was cleared to re-enter the dressing room as the blond beauty was adjusting her hat and skirt as she exited into the hallway. I didn't bother to ask for any details, however, I did discover Bobby wearing nothing but a towel when I walked back in. Did I really need to ask?

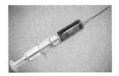

High Maintenance Hotties

Occasionally, backstage chicks can actually be too attractive. Some are so accustomed to being given everything in life because of their looks that they're just not worth the aggravation. Bobby had one such high-maintenance hottie come to the Indianapolis show in 2008.

This particular girl was one of Bobby's frequent female guests. I was familiar with her from previous tours and I remembered she was always arrogant and demanding. This time she phoned Bobby an hour prior to her backstage arrival. She informed him that she was running late and would require a private dressing room in which to prepare for the show. Bobby, however, set her straight. He informed the "princess" she was out of line and suggested she could get dressed in his bathroom or stay home.

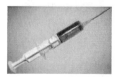

I tagged a bevy of great-looking backstage, after-show babes for Bobby in Richmond, Virginia on August 13, 2008. These girls were also "too attractive" and conducted themselves as if they were too good to wait around for multi-platinum rock stars. Granted, it was an outdoor event and the backstage amenities were few, but I tried to make their wait as comfortable as possible, offering the girls sodas and bottled water. When they began complaining about the long wait after only ten minutes and then asked to see a wine list, I suggested they would have a better time at Bret's formal meet-and-greet being held at a club on the other side of town. They opted to take my advice.

Kalyn and Stephanie are two girls I met on tour who were actually cool.

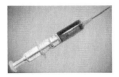

In August 2008 I met a woman named Rachel backstage at the PNC Amphitheater in New Jersey. With her long, jet-black hair, olive skin and voluptuous shape, this girl was a knock-out and looked to be of Italian descent. Although she seemed to be familiar with everyone in the band, I think she was the personal guest of one of the guys from the crew. Bubbly and energetic, Rachel bounced from bus to bus, hanging out with any middle-aged guy she could find who played a guitar and wore make-up. As Bobby was boarding his bus in the backstage lot, the girl asked him where he was going. "I'm gonna go suck my dick," he fired back. "Wanna join me?" Those within earshot, laughed hysterically at Bobby's vulgar comment as the young woman happily followed Bobby onto his bus.

"I'm gonna go suck my dick. Wanna join me?"

Bobby Dall, August 2008

I saw quite a bit of Rachel over the next several days. This was fine with me. She seemed cool, and in my opinion was one of the hottest of 2008's "tag-along" crop. Then one night, after having received VIP treatment all week, she got shitty with me. It was one of those nights when the guys just weren't seeing anyone after the show. She really wanted to see Bobby, but it wasn't going to happen. With her backstage pass around her neck and Budweiser on her breath, she demanded to see Bobby. I explained that he was dealing with a family matter that night. "Bullshit!" she exclaimed. She further suggested Bobby was rude for not seeing her. No longer caring how hot she was, I placed my finger in her face and instructed the Italian beauty to "back the fuck up" and "shut her mouth." This was following a show where I had been dealing with obnoxious, non-stop backstage chick attitudes all night. At that moment I was in no mood for any more creepy, stalker shit. She ultimately found someone else's bus to hang out on.

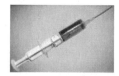

Heartbreaking

Not all interactions with fans are freaky. Some can rip your heart out. Poison was performing at the Oneida Casino in Green Bay, Wisconsin on Tuesday, June 20, 2006 and the hotel we were staying in was adjacent to the casino. Bobby and I had just finished lunch at the hotel's restaurant that afternoon and we were headed back to our room. As we walked through the lobby, Bobby was approached by a grandmotherly-looking woman who asked Bobby to say "hello" to her son. Bobby agreed and walked around the corner to where her family was waiting. We quickly discovered her thirty-something son was seriously handicapped. The young man's body, or what there was of it, was laying on a gurney. His body consisted only of a head and torso and was draped in a Poison concert T-shirt. An electronic device allowed him to breathe and he could barely speak. In fact, the only the word we could make out was "Poison" when his mother asked him to name his favorite band. Bobby gladly signed autographs for the family and offered them all free VIP tickets and after-show backstage passes. As we approached the elevator, once again heading back to our room and out of the family's view, Bobby had to stop and wipe tears from his eyes. I'd never seen the big, bad rock star so moved by anything before.

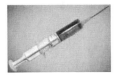

On another occasion while onstage in 2006, Bobby spotted a girl in the audience who was confined to a wheelchair. She was located in the nosebleed section. Bobby got the attention of the venue's security and had the handicapped woman brought up to the front row.

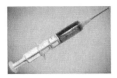

The Pot or the Kettle

Despite maligning the very people who've made them millions, some rock stars can be "creepy" fans themselves. Bobby once told me that as a diehard Rolling Stones fan, he would never dare ask for an autograph if he were to meet Mick Jagger or Keith Richards. However, in 2006 Bobby's girlfriend Meghan confessed to me that Bobby had a serious man-crush on Alice Cooper. "Don't let him fool you," Meghan told me. She further confessed that Bobby became tongue-tied when in Alice's presence. Very interesting.

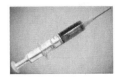

VIP Lounge

I enjoyed meeting the various nightly VIPs who came backstage while I was out with Poison. In the northeast we'd often run into such celebs as VH-1 host Eddie Trunk and comedian Craig Gass. While in New Jersey we always saw C.C. Banana, a comedian known for interviewing music personalities while doing a voice impression of C.C. DeVille, dressed in a banana suit. Hilarious! I love Mr. Banana. He's one of my all-time favorite backstage regulars. In Nashville, Mark Slaughter and the guys from Cinderella usually stopped by to say "hello." Of course in LA you never knew who was going to show up. One night in Florida, rapper-turned-rocker Vanilla Ice came backstage after the show.

C.C. DeVille with C.C. Banana backstage in 2001. (Photo by Kiva Kamerling)

Sometimes celebrities themselves are the most difficult Poison fans to deal with. In Chicago during the 2006 tour I was informed one of the members of the band Enuff Z'nuff had caused a scene with venue security. He reportedly was demanding to see Bobby over his poor seat location.

Me and Zak backstage in LA with Pretty Boy Floyd frontman,
Steve "Sex" Summers on July 1, 2006

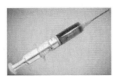

Another challenging backstage VIP regular is Erik Bleaman, aka "High Pitch." Erik is a large man with a very high-pitched voice. He's known nationwide as a frequent guest on Howard Stern's radio program. Erik typically likes to come to multiple shows on any given Poison tour. As a longtime Howard Stern fan I was thrilled to meet Erik backstage at the Jones Beach Amphitheater in Wantagh, New York while I was working the 2006 tour. I gave him my cell phone number and email address and told him to contact me if he ever needed anything.

219

Erik doesn't like to simply attend a show. He wants tickets and VIP passes. He also expects to hang out backstage before the show and on Bret's bus after the show. And he expects to introduce the band onstage. Being a rookie, I had no idea the guy had such demands when I gave him my contact info.

I thought it was odd that he immediately began calling *me* to ask for tickets and such. Sure, I gave him my number, but he was a radio celebrity and I was the bottom feeder on the Poison food chain. I assumed he had better contacts than me within the organization.

I soon discovered why *I* was now receiving his calls. Apparently following the 2006 Jones Beach show, Erik and his buddy were allowed on Bret's bus. Along with various babes, Erik and his pal witnessed a spirited night of partying. However, Erik's friend videoed much of the night's activities and posted the footage the following day on YouTube. Bret was pissed about this invasion of privacy. Immediately, Erik's Poison contacts became less enthusiastic about honoring his requests. I was unaware of any of this while on tour with the band in 2007. I only knew that for some reason Erik was bombarding me with email and cell phone requests for tickets and passes. When he arrived at the June 26 show in Wallingford, Connecticut Erik discovered only limited access after-show passes for Bobby's meet-and-greet accompanying his tickets at the box office — as opposed to his usual laminated all-access credentials. Clearly upset by this, Erik began calling my cell phone repeatedly to complain. I had to do something to appease Erik because I had a job to do and I couldn't have him calling me every five minutes. But I couldn't get a straight answer from anyone on the production staff as to why Erik had been "demoted." Finally, 2007 tour manager Larry Morand leveled with me, admitting that because of the YouTube issue, Bret no longer wanted Erik hanging around. The band would now only offer tickets to the radio personality. Since after-show passes technically guarantee nothing, they were included with Erik's tickets that night only as a PR measure. Erik was very upset over not being able to see Bret before or after that night's show, however Bobby did personally acknowledge Erik at that night's meet-and-greet.

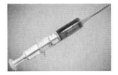

During the 2007 tour we were graced backstage in Connecticut and Pennsylvania with the presence of illusionist David Martin. With shoulder-length, curly brown hair and standing approximately five-foot-six, Martin looks like a younger version of rock singer Ronnie James Dio. For two nights, Poison members could barely turn around backstage without Martin invading their personal space. In the catering room, there he was, forcing C.C. to endure his mind-numbing card tricks. Outside by the tour buses, there he was again, sticking a deck of cards in Bobby's face. I've seen many people backstage over the years hocking their bands and books and so on, but this guy's in-your-face presence was truly over-the-top. I was not surprised when Martin made an infamous 2008 appearance on the popular TV show, *America's Got Talent*. After boldly describing his style as "very cutting edge" and announcing to America he was "ready to rock the world of magic," he botched what appeared to be the standard cut-

my-assistant-in-half routine. The performance quickly turned into a comedy act when Martin attempted to convince the show's judges that he hadn't bungled the trick at all, he was merely "playing with their minds."

C.C.'s assistant Brian Young (L) watches as illusionist David Martin dazzles C.C. backstage with one of his mind-numbing card tricks during the 2007 tour. (Photo by Missy Gilliam)

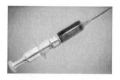

One band that is unanimously worshiped by Poison members is Cheap Trick. As I mentioned, "Talk Dirty to Me" sounds like a blatant rip-off of the 1982 Cheap Trick hit, "She's Tight." So it suffices to say the admiration runs pretty deep.

"I'm so happy that Cheap Trick is in the world, you know. I'm happy that Bun E. Carlos is in the world."

Rikki Rockett, September 2003

I was with Bobby in his dressing room in Nashville, Tennessee during the 2006 tour. Suddenly, Kevin Carter came bursting through the door. "Your Cheap Trick boy is in catering," Carter gleefully reported. Realizing I was a huge fan, Carter had mentioned to me the night before that Cheap Trick bassist Tom Petersson would be coming to the Nashville show. I instructed Kevin to alert me immediately upon his arrival.

Upon hearing this news, Bobby became somewhat frantic. He grabbed his bass, sat down and began feverishly plucking away. "Tom Petersson's here," he exclaimed. "I gotta get real good, real fast!" Bobby's anxieties were well placed. Petersson was more than just the bassist in a legendary pop group. He is a legend. Considered by many enthusiasts as the Thomas Edison of bass players, Petersson invented the twelve-string bass in the 1970s, single-handedly redefining the future role and sound of the modern rock bass player.

As I entered the backstage catering area, C.C., who also shared my passion for Cheap Trick, took me by the arm, walked me over and introduced me to Petersson. For a diehard rock dork like myself, to be introduced to Tom Petersson by C.C. DeVille was almost more than I could handle.

Twelve-string bass enthusiast Bobby Mattingly (L) with twelve-string bass creator Tom Petersson (R). (Photo courtesy of Bobby Mattingly)

The twelve-string bass was invented by Cheap Trick's Tom Petersson. (Photo courtesy of Bobby Mattingly)

"(Cheap Trick's album) Heaven Tonight changed my life."

C.C. DeVille, June 2006

I complimented Petersson on his group's new record *Rockford* that was just released. He seemed surprised, even doubtful that I had actually managed to get a copy of *Rockford* while in the middle of a tour. However, I dispelled any doubts he had when I immediately pulled my copy of the CD from my travel bag right there on the spot. It was an awesome experience. And yes, I was "creepy" enough to ask him to sign my CD!

I couldn't help but ask Tom Petersson to autograph my copy of Cheap Trick's *Rockford* CD.

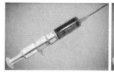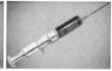

CHAPTER FIFTEEN

LIFE GOES ON - 2009 and beyond

"I just can't take your disabilities anymore," Bobby confessed on the phone in June when he informed me that I would not be involved in Poison's 2009 tour with Def Leppard and Cheap Trick.

I was becoming increasingly concerned for Bobby's well-being following the 2008 tour. His slurred ramblings were making phone conversations difficult and our face-to-face dialogues often resulted in him nodding off in mid-sentence.

Sadly, given his perception of me being a bumbling, incompetent fool, I had no influence over him. Bobby was dealing with some serious personal troubles and there was nothing I could do to help him.

I cautiously tried to reach out to his band members in early 2009. I had communications with both C.C. and Rikki regarding my concerns for Bobby. I didn't want to be a "drama queen" but I felt like I had to say something. C.C. thanked me for my concern and assured me that he would make plans to come to Florida and help his long-time friend.

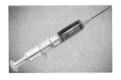

For years I had enjoyed hanging out with Bobby at his place several nights a week. In 2008 he transformed the guest room in his house into a rehearsal studio. On several occasions he and I would have impromptu jam sessions — cranking out our favorite classics by Ted Nugent, Judas Priest and AC/DC. These jams were usually a prelude to watching episodes of *Boston Legal* or one of Bobby's latest Blu-ray DVDs. However, these once fun evenings were becoming a drag.

In late 2008 Bobby and I made arrangements to meet at his ex-wife's house in Melbourne so I could borrow a piece of lighting gear. Our signals got crossed and we missed each other. I waited as long as I could for him, but I was late for one of my own gigs and I had to leave. A few moments later Bobby called me while I was en route to the club in which I was performing that night. "I love you, man," he told me with a disgusted tone. "But I gotta tell ya, sometimes you're a fucking moron!" Wow.

Early in 2009 Bobby mentioned to me that he was considering buying a gun. At that point I realized I'd finally had enough. It wasn't fun anymore. It was becoming stupid and potentially dangerous. The way I saw it, it was just a matter of time before things really got out of hand.

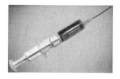

Bret's popular reality TV show returned to VH-1 on January 4. Despite a modified title, *Rock of Love Bus* offered the same "lonely rocker looking for love" premise as the two previous seasons. However, by season three the storyline had become so dopey and predictable, even I had lost interest in tuning in to see which skank he'd be tonguing from week to week. In fact, after only two or three episodes into season three, Bobby referred to the show as "an embarrassment."

During the production of the show's third season, on September 28, 2008, the driver of the truck hauling equipment for the show reportedly fell asleep at the wheel on I-57 in Illinois and struck two oncoming vehicles. Tragically, the accident took the lives of two nineteen-year-old college women and seriously injured two others. The driver worked for the show's production company and was not an employee of Bret's. However, Bret did temporarily suspend his participation in the show's production as he tried to reach out to the victims' families.

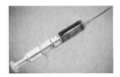

Then there was the "smack" heard around the world. Poison's music had recently been used in the hit Broadway production, *Rock of Ages,* and they were invited to perform as part of the opening number at the 63rd annual Tony Awards ceremony in New York on Sunday, June 7. The gala was broadcast live on CBS. The band's now-infamous performance consisted of a lip-synched, one minute version of their hit, "Nothin' But a Good Time." At the end of the performance, Bobby and C.C. rejoined Rikki on the drum riser for the big finish. Taking one bow too many, Bret made his way back to the riser a second or two too late — just in time to get thwacked in the head and knocked to the ground by a piece of scenery being lowered for the next number. The difference between this and Poison's equally infamous performance at the 1991 MTV awards was that in 2009, thanks to YouTube, Bret's mishap was immediately available for the world to see, over and over again.

Bret performing solo in 2009. (Photo by Monica Ciptak)

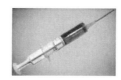

Bobby Dall onstage at New York's Jones Beach Amphitheater in 2004.
(Photo by Jennifer Berman)

During a sushi lunch meeting in early 2009 Bobby expressed to me how delighted he was to be touring with Cheap Trick bassist Tom Petersson. He immediately began calling off the names of other rock bassists who would be on his all-time "Greatest Bassist" list. In addition to Petersson, Bobby's list included Duff McKagan from Guns N' Roses, Aerosmith's Tom Hamilton and original Van Halen bassist Michael Anthony. I had to laugh when the name of legendary jazz bassist Stanley Clarke came into the conversation. "Stanley Clarke sucks," Bobby muttered from the passenger seat of my mini-van as I drove him home from the restaurant. "He doesn't make the list."

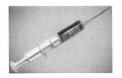

229

Bret onstage at New York's Jones Beach Amphitheater in 2004.
(Photo by Jennifer Berman)

Despite my desire to stay clear of the tour, I did make one brief outing in 2009. I visited Poison during their days off prior to their August 18 show in New Orleans, Louisiana.

In recent years, Bobby had a daily rental car available to transport him around various cities during downtime and days off while on tour. Wary of daily rental costs, he requested that his hometown assistant, Amber Curtis, bring his personal vehicle from Florida to Louisiana. Bobby would then keep his car out with him for the remainder of the tour, either towing it behind his bus or having his current tour assistant, Brian Young, drive it from city-to-city. Amber (and the car) needed to be in New Orleans immediately. However, it seemed that the eleven hour journey from Melbourne to The Big Easy might be a bit much for Amber to handle alone, especially since she had recently been dealing with a huge workload and gone several days with minimal sleep. Consequently, I accompanied her on the trip in order to insure that both the girl and car arrived safely. We arrived on Sunday, August 16. I would fly home after Tuesday night's show at the New Orleans Arena and Amber would remain with the tour for a week before flying back home. After careful consideration, Bobby ultimately opted for me to drive his car back to Florida.

Amber and Bobby in 2004. (Photo courtesy of Amber Curtis)

Upon arriving at our New Orleans hotel, I received a disturbing welcome from Bobby. I'm no psychologist but I immediately recognized that he wasn't himself. I knew Bobby back in Poison's platinum party days and his behavior in New Orleans was bizarre even by those standards. Wearing only a bath towel, Bobby approached me in Brian Young's hotel room and embraced me in a one-armed bear hug. He pressed his mouth against my ear and began whispering that I had meddled in his personal life and the lives of his children. I made clear that I had no idea what the hell he was talking about. He further insisted that I owed him an apology.

"An apology for what? Being your friend?" I asked.

"Yes," he replied.

He then pushed me down on the hotel bed. Standing before me, wearing only the aforementioned bath towel, he stretched his arms out like Jesus and commanded me to apologize. Believe me, at that moment I truly was sorry for offering him my friendship and I was all too happy to apologize.

"You are forgiven," he replied. "It's all in the past. And with that, I bid you a good evening."

He then grabbed Amber, pulled her into his adjacent hotel room and locked himself in for the night.

I looked at Brian Young and asked, "What the fuck was that?"

"You're lucky," he replied. "You got here on a good night."

Fortunately, my room was on the opposite side of the hotel so I could escape much of the subsequent madness. At times during my New Orleans visit Bobby seemed to be reaching an emotional breaking point. At other times he appeared more like his old self again — kinda. One thing's for sure, his erratic behavior throughout the tour had everyone in the band's organization walking on eggshells.

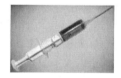

But my New Orleans experience wasn't completely traumatic. Rikki invited me to join in on a private late night tour of infamous ghost houses throughout the French Quarter.

It was about 10PM on Monday, August 17. Dressed and primped, I went down to the hotel lobby looking for some late night action. There I ran into Rikki and his assistant Bobby Tango. They apprised me of their plans and invited me to tag along. Rikki was apparently producing an independent film on vampires, so a tour of New Orleans's spooky side would prove to be a fun as well as valuable experience. Within a few seconds, a cab pulled up in front of the hotel to whisk me, Rikki, Tango, keyboardist Will Doughty and a couple of friends to the heart of the French Quarter. Dressed in a three piece tuxedo, our tour guide René showed us various haunted dwellings and the sites of legendary murders. Tango videotaped the event while Rikki interviewed René at various stops along the way. For me it was a fascinating evening. Given his layers of heavy clothing, I expected René to pass out in the sweltering late night summer heat, however, he pulled through like a true pro.

I was amazed that even in the dark backstreets of the French Quarter, people still recognized Rikki. One guy who presented himself as a musician shouted derogatory remarks from outside a blues club as we passed by. Another excited male fan made drumming gestures and gave an enthusiastic thumbs-up while blowing kisses at Rikki through the window of the restaurant where we enjoyed a late pizza dinner at 1AM.

But Rikki is very comfortable with his celebrity status. And it was refreshing to see that he doesn't take himself too seriously either. In fact, on the night of our ghoulish outing, Rikki sported a T-shirt which read, "Has Been."

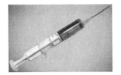

Sometimes you can be on a tour with someone and still seem a million miles away. In fact, you stand a better chance of seeing Jesus backstage at a Poison concert than you do running into Bret Michaels. So I wasn't surprised to only briefly bump into him on his way to the stage just prior to show time in New Orleans.

I *was* disappointed by not being able to spend any time with C.C. while I was in New Orleans. We spoke on the phone on Sunday evening shortly after I arrived at the hotel and he informed me that he was already out for the night with friends. Unfortunately, my plans to join C.C. and his entourage on Bourbon Street later in the evening were foiled when I received a text message from Amber summoning me back to the hotel as I was en route to the legendary party spot. C.C. called me the following night and *I* was the one who was out and about while *he* was back at the hotel. We agreed to get together later, however by the time I returned to the hotel at 2AM, he'd already crashed for the night. Sadly, I only had an opportunity to shake hands and say "hello" to him on our way to the buses following Poison's Tuesday night performance. Before Def Leppard was half way through their set I was already in Bobby's car, headed back to Florida.

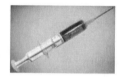

I received a phone call from Craig Gass late at night on August 25. Craig is a well-known comedian who works the stand-up circuit and makes frequent TV appearances on *Comedy Central* as well as morning radio programs like *The Howard Stern Show* and *The Mancow Show*. Also known for his spot-on impersonations of such rock icons as Gene Simmons, Paul Stanley and former Skid Row frontman Sebastian Bach, Craig has been friends with Bobby for years and we also developed a friendship after first meeting in Connecticut on Poison's 2006 tour. Typically, I'm up late most nights so I don't know how I managed to miss his call. But when I finally did hear Craig's voicemail the following morning I was disturbed by the news he had to share. Craig had attended the Def Leppard/Poison show that night at the USANA Amphitheatre in Salt Lake City, Utah. When Poison hit the stage (late), Craig was alarmed to discover that Bobby was nowhere on stage. In fact, Bobby's slot was surprisingly being filled by Bon Jovi bassist, Hugh McDonald. Metalsludge.tv reported that it had been announced at the show that Bobby was too "ill" to perform that night. That was putting it mildly.

When Poison arrived in Utah, Bobby chose to go to his ski home rather than remain with the entourage at the venue. Details regarding the rest of the day's events differ from one tour staff member to the next, however, as show time approached, Bobby was still at his house. Reportedly McDonald stepped up to help out with the show and received a last minute, backstage, crash course in playing a handful of Poison hits. And to my knowledge, for the first time in their history, Poison performed live without Bobby Dall.

Upon receiving Craig's message, I immediately called Amber. This was the first she had heard of the incident and began to panic. At that point we didn't know where Bobby was or if he was even alive. I then began calling members of the Poison organization to get more information. Only Rikki Rockett took my call. He offered little information other than expressing extreme disgust over the situation. I received a call later in the day from one of Poison's stage techs and he acted as if he had no idea what I was talking about. Fortunately, Amber was able to get through to C.C. and we learned that Bobby was okay, more or less. He finally arrived at the venue the night before shortly after Poison had finished their set and he was now back with the entourage, headed for the next show in Albuquerque, New Mexico.

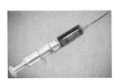

CHAPTER FIFTEEN

In 2006 he chastised me publicly and privately for temporarily leaving the tour when I became ill and needed to seek treatment. He viewed not completing a tour as a sign of weakness. Although Bobby leaving the tour early made the most sense for all involved, he desperately wanted to fulfill his professional obligation. By the time the band arrived in California, a few days after Salt Lake City, he clearly couldn't go on. A private jet was chartered to bring him back to Florida and Cinderella bassist Eric Brittingham was recruited to complete the last two week's worth of dates on Poison's tour.

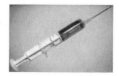

On a happier note, Rikki Rockett and his wife Melanie celebrated the birth of their first child in 2009. Weighing in at seven pounds and four ounces, Jude Aaron Rockett entered the world at 4:31AM on July 14. Cinderella drummer Fred Coury filled in for Rikki on the Poison tour for several days until he returned from maternity leave.

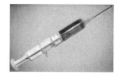

2009 was also personally eventful. In addition to frantically trying to keep up with various book deadlines, I spent much of the year writing for Ink19.com, reviewing Central Florida concerts from such acts as Papa Roach, the New York Dolls, Queensryche, and Jeffree Star. Also, in 2009 my band Dead Serios staged a couple of successful and highly publicized Florida reunion shows. Proving the old saying that "the apple doesn't fall far from the tree," my now sixteen-year-old son Jesse debuted on Florida club and concert stages as the drummer in his own band, The Ellers, named after his high school phys. ed. coach, Greg Eller. In July they recorded a remake of Poison's 1986 classic, "Look What the Cat Dragged In."

At forty-six, I was still making local headlines in 2009 with my longtime band Dead Serios.
(Photo by Kevin Roberts)

My sixteen-year-old son Jesse (top left) debuted in 2009 as the drummer in own band, The Ellers.

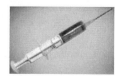

So, here I am in January 2010, reflecting on my experiences over the last twenty years with Poison. When they first hit the scene, I was hardly a fan. However, I was later seduced by the irresistible combination of Bret Michaels's rock star charisma, C.C. Deville's guitar riffs, the showmanship of Rikki Rockett and the rock-ribbed dedication of Bobby Dall. I would have done anything to become part of their world. In the end, my dream came true. I graduated from the back row of their sold-out concerts in the late 1980s to their often outrageous, backstage after-show parties in the early 1990s.

As a writer in the 2000s, I established a deeper personal bond with the band and I was ultimately invited into their inner sanctum. But when my dream came true, the actual experience fell short of my naïve expectations. Rock and roll is largely an illusion of perpetual fun, excitement and spontaneity. In reality, it's often monotonous, predictable, and at times, sheer drudgery. What really makes it difficult is having to carefully navigate around the potential minefield of volatile personalities and outsized egos that can blow up at any moment.

Over the years I've seen the members of Poison at their best and I've seen them at their worst. Consequently, along the way I lost my once innocent, wide-eyed fascination with the music business. I no longer have any interest in meeting any rock stars and my once burning desire to experience life on the road has been extinguished. In all honesty, just the sight of a tour bus now makes my stomach feel a bit queasy.

But I wouldn't go back and change a thing (okay, maybe I would change a few things). I've seen places I would have never seen, I met people who I would have never met, I connected with some incredible women and I learned a few valuable life lessons — all while working for one of my favorite bands. Not many people can say that. Despite hitting the occasional pothole along the way, I do appreciate being brought along for the ride.

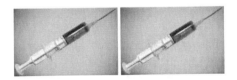

About the Author

For the last thirty years author Christopher Long has led the life that most rock and roll fans can only dream of. His twenty year relationship with the multi-platinum-selling band *Poison* combined with his vast experience as a music journalist, musician, independent record producer, concert promoter and nightclub DJ makes him an acknowledged rock and roll expert and insider.

Since 1985, this award-winning entertainer has performed in his own band, Dead Serios -- opening for such chartbusting groups as Marilyn Manson, Hootie and the Blowfish, Faith No More, Anthrax, Cinderella and Slaughter.

As a concert promoter, Long booked his first national act (a Journey-type group called Aaron) in 1978 at the age of fifteen while attending DeLaura Junior High School in Satellite Beach, Florida. By the 1990s he was responsible for bringing groups like Marilyn Manson, Faster Pussycat and The Southern Rock All-Stars to clubs and concert stages throughout Florida's Space Coast.

As a journalist, Long has spent considerable time in the last decade traveling with and interviewing various rock headliners. He is considered by many to be a leading authority on rock and roll and his lively columns and reviews are read each month online as well as in various Florida entertainment publications. He has also written official bios for musical artists including Poison and the band's frontman, Bret Michaels, star of the VH-1 reality show, *Rock of Love*. But his vast musical knowledge and experience is not limited to just rock and roll. In 2004, country music's chart-topping sister duo The Kinleys had also incorporated Long's work into their official press kit.

In addition to keeping in tune with current pop, hip hop and dance trends as one of Florida's East Coast top nightclub, party and special event DJ/Personalities, Long also hosts the Brevard Live Music Awards ceremony held annually in Melbourne, Florida.

In many ways, Christopher Long's experiences are quite similar to that of award-winning filmmaker and journalist Cameron Crowe, in the early 1970s. However, even today Long continues to live in rock's fast lane. Now, many of his amazing tales can finally be shared with rock and roll fans around the world.